Québécois-English
English-Québécois

Dictionary & Phrasebook

Dictionary & Phrasebooks

Albanian

Arabic (Eastern)

Australian

Azerbaijani

Basque

Bosnian

Breton

British

Cajun

Chechen

Croatian

Danish

Esperanto

French

Georgian

German

Greek

Hebrew *romanized & script*

Igbo

Ilocano

Irish

Italian

Japanese *romanized*

Lao *romanized*

Lingala

Malagasy

Maltese

Pilipino (Tagalog)

Polish

Québécois

Romanian

Romansch

Russian

Shona

Slovak

Somali

Spanish (Latin American)

Swahili

Swedish

Tajik

Thai *romanized*

Turkish

Ukrainian

Québécois-English
English-Québécois

Dictionary & Phrasebook

Renata Isajlovic & Isabelle Martin

Hippocrene Books, Inc.
New York

ISBN 0-7818-0920-7

For information, address:
Hippocrene Books, Inc.
171 Madison Avenue
New York, NY 10016

Cataloging in Publication Data available from the
Library of Congress.

Printed in the United States of America.

CONTENTS

CONTENTS

INTRODUCTION

French is one of Canada's two official languages. Although French-speaking communities are found throughout the country, the largest French-speaking population resides in Quebec. Various cultural, historical and political factors have had such an impact on the evolution of the French language in Canada that the French dialects spoken throughout the country vary greatly.

French first appeared in North America in 1534 when French explorer Jacques Cartier claimed the continent for France. Settlers who colonized New France spoke various dialects, depending on where they were originally from in France (e.g. Normandy, Burgundy). Because they needed to be able to communicate with each other, the settlers chose French as their new *lingua franca*.

French in Quebec differed from French in France from the start. Settlers coined expressions to describe new realities such as harsh winters and adopted Aboriginal words to describe such things as North American wildlife (e.g. *ouananiche* and *maskinongé* are two types of fish, and *atoca* means cranberry).

It was only after the British Conquest of 1759 that French in Quebec truly became distinct. As French settlers in North America were now isolated from their fatherland, their language evolved differently than the one spoken by their European cousins. This explains why certain words that were abandoned long ago in France are still used in Quebec today. And one must not forget the undeniable impact English has had on Québécois French, with words such as *binnes* (beans) and *bécosses* (backhouse) creeping into the language.

The French Revolution in 1789 also had a significant impact on French spoken in France, with the bourgeoisie now setting the standard for proper French. However, because French settlers had no contact with France, they continued to speak the King's French. This helps explain the difference between French accents heard in Quebec and France.

Today, the survival of the French culture and language in Canada is ensured by Canada's Official Languages Act, which supports the development of French and English linguistic minorities in Canada, and by Quebec's Charter of the French Language, which guarantees the predominance of French over other languages in Quebec and makes French the language of work and business in the province.

ABBREVIATIONS

adj.	adjective
adv.	adverb
conj.	conjunction
f.	feminine
inf.	informal
n.	noun
m.	masculine
pl.	plural
prep.	preposition
pron.	pronoun
qué.	Québécois (indicates that the word is not used in standard French (France) or that it has a different meaning in Quebec)
sing.	singular
slang	slang
v.	verb

QUÉBÉCOIS ALPHABET

Letter	Name of letter
a	[ah]
b	[bay]
c	[say]
d	[day]
e	[euh]
f	[eff]
g	[zhay]
h	[ash]
i	[ee]
j	[zhee]
k	[kah]
l	[el]
m	[em]
n	[en]
o	[oh]
p	[pay]
q	[koo]
r	[err]
s	[ess]
t	[tay]
u	[oo]
v	[vay]
w	[doobleuh-vay]
x	[ix]
y	[ee-grek]
z	[zed]

PRONUNCIATION GUIDE

Consonants	Québécois example	Approximate English equivalent
b	**balle** ball	ball
c (soft c before e, i, y)	**cil** eyelash	dance
c (hard c before a, o, u)	**canot** canoe	canoe
ç (always soft)	**garçon** boy	silk
d	**demain** tomorrow	day
f	**ferme** farm	farm
g (soft g before e, i, y)	**genre** gender	s in leisure
g (hard g before a, o, u)	**golf** golf	golf
h (always silent)	**horloge** clock	—
j	**jour** day	s in leisure
k	**kilt** kilt	kilt
l	**long** long	long
m	**matin** morning	morning
n	**navire** ship	navy
p	**porte** door	peach
q	**quille** bowling pin	kilt
r	**renard** fox	restaurant
s	**salon** living room	silk
s (between vowels)	**prison** jail	zoo
t	**tomate** tomato	tomato

v	**vision** vision	vision
w	**wagon** wagon	vision
x	**examen** exam	exam
	exceller to excel	excel
z	**zoo** zoo	zoo

N.B. French consonants are generally not pronounced at the end of a word.

e.g. *beaucoup* is pronounced *bo-koo*, not *bo-koop*

This rule does not apply to the letters **c**, **f**, **l**, **q**, and **r**, and the consonant cluster **ng**.

Vowel	Québécois example	Approximate English equivalent
a, à	**avion** airplane	cat
â	**gâteau** cake	father
e	**premier** first	berth
é	**école** school	day
è, ê	**crème** cream	berry
i, î	**île** island	key
i (before vowel)	**lieu** place	yes
o	**sol** ground	hot
	pot pot	coat
ô	**dôme** dome	coat
u, ù, û	**bûche** log	no equivalent in English; say *ee* and round your lips

Nasal vowels*	Québécois example	Approximate English equivalent
an, am, en, em	**enfant** child	Hans
ien	**lien** link	no equivalent in English; *y* + *ain* in **train** (short final n)
in, ein, ain, aim	**vin** wine	train (short final n)
ion	**lion** lion	no equivalent in English; *y* + *on* in **bonbon** (short final n)
oin	**foin** hay	no equivalent in English; *w* + *ain* in **train** (short final n)
on, om	**maison** house	bonbon (short final n)
un, um	**parfum** perfume	no equivalent in English; say *uh* + *n*

*The *n* or *m* following nasal vowels is not fully pronounced.

Other sounds	Québécois example	Approximate English equivalent
ai, aî	**balai** broom	berry
au, eau	**bateau** boat	coat
ch	**chien** dog	ship
eil, eille	**pareil** same	no equivalent in English; *e* in berry + *y*
er (at the end of a word)	**aller** to go	day
eu	**heureux** happy	berth
euil, euille	**fauteuil** armchair	no equivalent in English; *e* in berth + *y*
ez	**chez**	day
gn	**montagne** mountain	onion
ll	**oreille** ear **mille** thousand	yes long
ng	**camping** camping	camping
oi	**oiseau** bird	wagon
ou	**hibou** owl	hoop
ph	**telephone** telephone	telephone
qu	**quille** bowling pin	kilt
ui	**huile** oil	ween

BASIC QUÉBÉCOIS GRAMMAR

Word Order

Word order in Québécois is generally the same as in English, i.e. subject—verb—object.

Je / vois / un oiseau.   I / see / a bird.
S   V   Obj.   S   V   Obj.

However, when the object is replaced by a direct object pronoun, the word order is reversed and becomes subject—object—verb.

Je / le / vois. which is literally I / it / see.
S Obj. V   S Obj. V

Nouns

Gender

Before going any further, it is important to note that, in French, nouns are either masculine or feminine. Adjectives and past participles agree in both gender and number with the nouns they modify and/or describe. The same applies to articles preceding nouns.

Unfortunately, there is no rule for determining the gender of most nouns. Knowledge of other Latin languages such as Spanish may be helpful in guessing noun gender. However, keep in mind that this method is not foolproof. Many suggest that beginners memorize the indefinite article with the noun when learning vocabulary words.

une poire *n.f.*	a pear
un ananas *n.m.*	a pineapple

un raisin *n.m.*	a grape
une fraise *n.f.*	a strawberry

However, nouns describing an animate object have both a masculine and feminine form.

The feminine is usually formed by adding *e* at the end of the masculine noun.

un avocat *n.m.*	a male lawyer
une avocate *n.f.*	a female lawyer
un marchand *n.m.*	a male merchant
une marchande *n.f.*	a female merchant

When the masculine form ends in *e*, the spelling of the feminine form does not change; the article indicates the gender of the noun.

un comptable *n.m.*	a male accountant
une comptable *n.f.*	a female accountant

In most cases where the above-mentioned rules do not apply, the feminine is formed as follows:

masculine noun ending	feminine noun ending
-el	-elle
-en	-enne
-er	-ère
-et	-ette
-eur	-eure/-euse
-f	-ve
-on	-onne
-oux	-ouse
-teur	-teuse/-trice
-x	-se

Plural

As a rule of thumb, the plural of nouns is formed by adding an *s* at the end of the noun. It is important to remember that the *s* is not pronounced.

un enfant *n.m.*	a child
des enfants *n.m.pl.*	children

In cases where the previous rule does not apply, the plural is formed as follows:

singular noun ending	plural noun ending
-ail	-aux
-al	-aux
-au	-aux
-eau	-eaux
-eu	-eux
-s, -x, -z	same

Articles

There are three types of articles in French: definite, indefinite, and partitive.

Each type of article has three forms: masculine, feminine, and plural.

Definite articles

le (m.)   la (f.)
1. Both *le* and *la* change to *l'* when placed before a word beginning with a vowel and most words beginning with *h*.

les (pl.)
2. *Les* is used for all plural nouns, regardless of gender.

Indefinite articles

un (m.)   une (f.)   des (pl.)
1. *Des* is used for all plural nouns, regardless of gender.

Partitive articles

du (m.)   de la (f.)
1. *Du* changes to *d'* and *de la* to *de l'* when placed before a word beginning with a vowel and most words beginning with *h*.

des (pl.)
2. *Des* is used for all plural nouns, regardless of gender.

Adjectives

As mentioned earlier, adjectives agree in gender and number with the nouns they modify.

Feminine

As a rule of thumb, the feminine form of adjectives is formed by adding an *e* at the end of the masculine form.

	masculine form	feminine form
slow	lent	lente
pretty	joli	jolie

In cases where the previous rule does not apply, most feminine adjectives are formed as follows:

masculine form	feminine form
-eil	-eille
-el	-elle
-en	-enne
-er	-ère
-et	-ette
-eur	-euse
-eux	-euse
-on	-onne
-s	-sse
-teur	-trice

Plural

The plural form of adjectives is generally formed by adding an *s* to the masculine or feminine form of the adjective.

	masc.	masc. pl.	fem.	fem. pl.
slow	lent	lents	lente	lentes
pretty	joli	jolis	jolie	jolies

In cases where the previous rule does not apply, plural adjectives are formed as follows:

singular ending	plural ending
-al	-aux
-s or -x	same

When a feminine noun is paired with a masculine noun, the masculine plural forms of adjectives and past participles must be used.

Cette jupe (n.f.sing.) est bleue (adj.f.sing.).
This skirt is blue.

Ce foulard (n.m.sing.) est bleu (adj.m.sing.).
This scarf is blue.

Cette jupe (n.f.sing.) et ce foulard (n.m.sing.)
  sont bleus (adj.m.pl.).
This skirt and this scarf are blue.

The above grammar rule is applied when there is
at least one masculine noun in an enumeration.

Cette pomme (n.f.sing.), cette poire (n.f.sing.),
  cette pêche (n.f.sing.) et ce pamplemousse
  (n.m.sing.) sont juteux (adj.m.pl.).
**This apple, this pear, this peach and this
  grapefruit are juicy.**

Adverbs

Most adverbs are formed by adding *-ment* to the
feminine form of the corresponding adjective.

	masculine form	feminine form	adverb
slow	lent	lente	lentement
pretty	joli	jolie	joliement

Adverbs corresponding to adjectives ending in *-ant*
and *-ent* are formed as follows:

	masculine form	feminine form	adverb
mean	méchant	méchante	méchammant
obvious	évident	évidente	évidemment

Pronouns

Subject Pronouns

English	French
I	je
you	tu
he/it	il
she/it	elle
we	nous/on
you (pl.)	vous
they	ils/elles

• The subject pronoun *je* changes to *j'* when the verb that follows begins with a vowel or an *h*.

e.g. j'aime, j'haïs

• In Quebec, the subject pronoun *on* is often used instead of *nous*. It is conjugated like *il* and *elle* (3rd person singular).

• As in standard French, there exists a distinction between formal and informal usage of the subject pronoun you, i.e. *tu* and *vous*.

The subject pronoun *vous* is not only the plural form of *tu*, but is also used in formal address. *Vous* should be used to address strangers and people met in formal settings. However, this is not as strict a rule in Quebec as it is in France. In Quebec, *tu* is more commonly used than *vous*, even in formal settings. One should therefore not take offense, as no disrespect is intended.

Direct object pronouns

English	French
me	me
you	te
him/it	le
her/it	la
us	nous
you (pl.)	vous
them	les

As mentioned in the Word Order section, a direct object pronoun replacing the object in a sentence is placed before the verb.

Je **le** vois.   which is literally I **it** see.

Indirect object pronouns

English	French
to me	me
to you	te
to him/it	lui
to her/it	lui
to us	nous
to you (pl.)	vous
to them	leur

Like the direct object pronoun, the indirect object pronoun is placed before the verb.

Je **leur** parle. which is literally I **to them** am talking.

When both direct and indirect object pronouns are used in a sentence, the direct object pronoun is placed before the indirect object pronoun.

| Elle **le lui** a prêté. | which is literally | She **it to him** lent. |

Reflexive pronouns

English	French
myself	me
yourself	te
himself/herself/itself	se
ourselves	nous
yourselves	vous
themselves	se

The reflexive pronoun is placed between the subject and the verb in a sentence; it must agree with the subject.

| Je **me** lave. | which is literally | I **myself** am washing. |

Possessive adjectives and pronouns

In the following table, the first form given is the adjective, followed by the pronoun.

English	masc. sing.	fem. sing.	masc. and fem. pl.
my	mon	ma	mes
my/ mine	mon/ mien	ma/ mienne	mes/miens, miennes
your(s)	ton/tien	ta/tienne	tes/tiens, tiennes

his/her(s)	son/sien	sa/sienne	ses/siens, siennes
our(s)	notre/ nôtre	notre/ nôtre	nos/ nôtres *m./f.*
your(s)	votre/ vôtre	votre/ vôtre	vos/ vôtres *m./f.*
their(s)	leur/leur	leur/leur	leurs/ leurs *m./f.*

The masculine adjective form is used with feminine nouns beginning with a vowel or an *h*.

e.g. **Mon** (masc. sing.) horloge (fem. sing.) est cassée.
My clock is broken.

Verbs

Verbs are grouped in three categories according to their endings in the infinitive. Group 1 consists of verbs ending in *-er*; Group 2 consists of verbs ending in *-ir* that are conjugated like *finir* (to finish); the remaining verbs make up Group 3. A verb book might be helpful, as there are many exceptions and irregular verbs in the latter category.

Verbs are conjugated by adding endings to the verb stem. To determine the stem of the verb, drop the ending from the infinitive form of the verb (e.g. *-er, -ir, -re, -oir*).

Present tense

	Group 1 -er danser (to dance)	Group 2 -ir finir (to finish)	Group 3 -re vendre (to sell)
je	danse	finis	vends
tu	danses	finis	vends
il/elle/on	danse	finit	vend
nous	dansons	finissons	vendons
vous	dansez	finissez	vendez
ils/elles	dansent*	finissent*	vendent*

*-ent is silent.

Past tense

The past tense is a compound tense formed using an auxiliary verb (either *avoir*/to have or *être*/to be) in the present tense and a past participle. The auxiliary verbs *avoir* and *être* are conjugated as follows:

	avoir (to have)	être (to be)
je/j'	ai	suis
tu	as	es
il/elle/on	a	est
nous	avons	sommes
vous	avez	êtes
ils/elles	ont	sont

Past participles are generally formed by dropping the ending of the infinitive form of the verb and adding the following:

infinitive ending	past participle
-er	é
-ir	i
-re	u

Past participles conjugated with *être* must agree in gender and number with the subject of the sentence. The feminine and plural forms of past participles generally take the same endings as adjectives (i.e. add *e* to form the feminine and *s* to form the plural).

Elle est entrée dans la chambre.
    She entered the room.
Ils sont devenus célèbres.
    They became famous.

Most verbs require *avoir* as their auxiliary verb in the past tense. However, because there is no rule for determining whether the past tense of a verb is formed with *avoir* or *être*, here is a short list of verbs requiring *être* in the past tense:

aller	to go
arriver	to arrive
devenir	to become
entrer	to enter
mourir	to die
naître	to be born
partir	to leave
sortir	to exit
venir	to come

All reflexive verbs, i.e. verbs in which the subject performs the action on himself/herself, are conjugated with *être* in the past tense. The reflexive pronoun *se* precedes the infinitive form of reflexive verbs, e.g. *se laver* (to wash oneself), *se dire* (to tell oneself).

Past participles conjugated with *avoir* do not agree with the subject of the sentence, but with the direct object when it is placed **before** the verb in the sentence.

Elle a mangé une pomme.
S   V   DO
  She ate an apple.
    S V   DO

La pomme qu'elle a mangée.
  DO   S   V
The apple that she ate.
    DO   S V

	Group 1 -er danser (to dance)	Group 2 -ir finir (to finish)	Group 3 -re vendre (to sell)
j'	ai dansé	ai fini	ai vendu
tu	as dansé	as fini	as vendu
il/elle/on	a dansé	a fini	a vendu
nous	avons dansé	avons fini	avons vendu
vous	avez dansé	avez fini	avez vendu
ils/elles	ont dansé	ont fini	ont vendu

Future tense

Like the present tense, the future tense is formed by adding endings to the verb stem. To determine the stem of the verb, drop the ending from the infinitive form of the verb (e.g. *-er, -ir, -re, -oir*).

	Group 1 -er danser (to dance)	Group 2 -ir finir (to finish)	Group 3 -re vendre (to sell)
je	danser**ai**	fini**rai**	vend**rai**
tu	danser**as**	fini**ras**	vend**ras**
il/elle/on	danser**a**	fini**ra**	vend**ra**
nous	danser**ons**	fini**rons**	vend**rons**
vous	danser**ez**	fini**rez**	vend**rez**
ils/elles	danser**ont**	fini**ront**	vend**ront**

Negation

Negation is formed by adding *ne* before the verb and another negative element immediately after the verb. In a compound tense, the second negative element is placed between the auxiliary verb and the past participle.

Je **ne** sais **pas**.	I do not know.
Je n'ai **pas** pu le faire.	I could not do it.
Je **ne** travaille **plus**.	I do not work anymore.
Elle **ne** sourit **jamais**.	She never smiles.

Other examples of negation are:

Ne ... **aucun**	Not any
Ne ... **pas encore**	Not yet
Ne ... **personne**	No one
Ne ... **rien**	Nothing

In spoken Québécois, *ne* is often dropped.

| Je sais **pas**. | I don't know. |
| J'ai **pas** pu le faire. | I couldn't do it. |

Questions

The easiest way to ask a question in French is to raise your voice at the end of a declarative sentence, as you would do in English.

e.g. **Tu as acheté ton billet?**
     You bought your ticket?

You can also begin an interrogative sentence with *est-ce que*.

e.g. **Est-ce que tu as acheté ton billet?**
     Did you buy your ticket?

Finally, you can reverse the pronoun and verb to ask a question.

e.g. **As-tu acheté ton billet?**
     Have you bought your ticket?

Liaison

Final consonants are not pronounced unless followed by a word beginning with a vowel or silent *h*. The carrying over of the sound is called *liaison*.

Elle est amoureuse.   She is in love.

Here, the *t* carries over to *amoureuse*. The sentence is thus pronounced *el eh ta-moo-reuhz*.

When words end in *s* or *x*, a *z* sound is carried over; when they end in *d*, the sound carried over is *t*.

deux hommes (deuh zohm)   two men
grand arbre (granh tahrbr)   big tree

QUÉBÉCOIS-ENGLISH DICTIONARY

A

à *prep.* at; to; in; ~ **côté de** *prep.* beside, next to;
    ~ **travers** *prep.* across; through
abandonner *v.* abandon (to)
aboutir *v.* finish (to)
abracadabrant *adj.* astounding
abreuvoir *n.m. qué.* water fountain
abri *n.m.* shelter
abricot *n.m.* apricot
abriller (s') *v. qué.* cover oneself (to)
abriter *v.* shelter (to)
absolu *adj.* absolute
absurde *adj.* absurd, preposterous
abuser *v.* abuse (to)
accélérer *v.* accelerate (to)
accentuer *v.* accentuate (to)
acceptable *adj.* acceptable
accepter *v.* accept (to)
accommodant *adj.* easygoing; good-natured
accompagner *v.* accompany (to); escort (to)
accompli *adj.* accomplished
accomplir *v.* accomplish (to)
accorder (s') *v.* get along (to)
accueillant *adj.* welcoming
accueillir *v.* welcome (to); greet (to)
accuser *v.* accuse (to)
acéré *adj.* sharp
achalandé *adj.* popular (establishment); busy
achalant *adj. qué.* bothersome, annoying
achaler *v. qué.* bother (to)
acheté *adj.* bought, purchased
acheter *v.* buy (to), purchase (to)
acoustique *adj.* acoustic
acquérir *v.* acquire (to)
acquis *adj.* acquired
âcre *adj.* acrid

actif *adj.* active
activer *v.* activate (to)
addition *n.f.* bill; addition
additionner *v.* add (to) (numbers)
adéquat *adj.* adequate
adjacent *adj.* adjacent, neighboring
admettre *v.* admit (to)
administrer *v.* administer (to)
admirable *adj.* admirable
admirer *v.* admire (to)
admis *adj.* admitted, accepted
adon *n.m. qué.* coincidence
adonner (s') *v. qué.* get along (to)
adopter *v.* adopt (to)
adorer *v.* adore (to)
adresser *v.* address (to)
adroit *adj.* skillful
adulte *n.m.* adult
aéroport *n.m.* airport
affamé *adj.* hungry; famished
affilé *adj.* sharp
affiler *v.* sharpen (to)
affreux *adj.* hideous
africain *n.m.* African; *adj.* African
agaçant *adj.* aggravating, annoying
agacer *v.* irritate (to)
âgé *adj.* old
agenouiller (s') *v.* kneel (to)
agent de voyage *n.m.* travel agent
agile *adj.* agile; nimble
agir *v.* act (to); proceed (to)
agréable *adj.* pleasant
agricole *adj.* agricultural
aider *v.* help (to)
aigre *adj.* sour; tart
aigre-doux *adj.* sweet-and-sour; bittersweet
aigu *adj.* acute; sharp
aiguiser *v.* sharpen (to)
aimable *adj.* kind

aimé *adj.* loved
aimer *v.* love (to); like (to)
aîné *n.m.* elder; *adj.* eldest
air *n.m.* air; ~ **climatisé** *n.m.* air conditioning;
    ~ **conditionné** *n.m. qué.* air conditioning
ajouter *v.* add (to)
alcool *n.m.* alcohol
alcoolique *adj.* alcoholic
alcoolisé *adj.* alcoholic (beverage)
alerte *adj.* alert
allemand *n.m.* German; *adj.* German
aller *v.* go (to)
allonger (s') *v.* lie down (to)
allumer *v.* light (to); turn on (to)
allumette *n.f.* match
ambassade *n.f.* embassy
ambigu *adj.* ambiguous
ambitieux *adj.* ambitious
ambulance *n.f.* ambulance
amélioré *adj.* improved
amener *v.* bring (to)
amer *adj.* bitter
américain *n.m.* American; *adj.* American
ami *n.m.* friend; **petit** ~ *n.m.* boyfriend; **petite ~e**
    n.f. girlfriend
amour *n.m.* love
amoureux *adj.* loving
ample *adj.* broad
amusant *adj.* amusing
amuser *v.* amuse (to)
analgésique *adj.* analgesic
ananas *n.m.* pineapple
ancien *adj.* ancient; former
aneth *n.m.* dill
anglais *n.m.* English; *adj.* English
annoncer *v.* announce (to)
annuel *adj.* annual
anormal *adj.* abnormal
antiseptique *adj.* antiseptic

anxieux *adj.* anxious; uneasy
apercevoir *v.* perceive (to); glimpse (to)
apeuré *adj.* scared, frightened
aplatir *v.* flatten (to)
apparaître *v.* appear (to)
appartenir *v.* belong (to)
appel *n.m.* call
appeler *v.* call (to)
applaudir *v.* applaud (to)
appliquer *v.* apply (to)
apporter *v.* bring (to)
apprécier *v.* appreciate (to)
apprendre *v.* learn (to)
approcher *v.* approach (to)
approfondi *adj.* elaborate; thorough
approuver *v.* approve (to)
appuyer *v.* support (to)
après *adv.* after; *prep.* after
après-midi *n.m.* afternoon
arabe *n.m.* Arab, Arabic; *adj.* Arab, Arabian, Arabic
arbre *n.m.* tree
archaïque *adj.* archaic
architecture *n.f.* architecture
ardu *adj.* arduous
aréna *n.m.* arena
argent *n.m.* money; silver; *adj.* silver; ~ **comptant** *n.m.* cash
aride *adj.* arid
arracher *v.* tear out (to); pull out (to)
arranger *v.* arrange (to); repair (to) *inf.*
arrêter *v.* arrest (to); stop (to)
arriver *v.* arrive (to)
arrogant *adj.* arrogant
arroser *v.* water (to)
art *n.m.* art
artistique *adj.* artistic
asiatique *n.m.* Asian; *adj.* Asian
aspirateur *n.m.* vacuum cleaner
assembler *v.* assemble (to)

asseoir (s') *v.* sit (to)
assiette *n.f.* plate
assir (s') *v. qué.* sit (to)
assoiffé *adj.* thirsty
associer (s') *v.* associate (to) (oneself)
assurer *v.* assure (to); insure (to)
asteur *adv. qué.* now
astiner (s') *v. qué.* argue (to)
astronomie *n.f.* astronomy
astucieux *adj.* astute
athlétique *adj.* athletic
athlétisme *n.m.* track and field
atoca *n.f. qué.* cranberry
attacher *v.* attach (to)
attaquer *v.* attack (to)
atteindre *v.* reach (to)
attendre *v.* wait (to)
attirer *v.* attract (to); entice (to); lure (to)
attraper *v.* catch (to)
aubergine *n.f.* eggplant
augmenter *v.* increase (to); raise (to)
aujourd'hui *adv.* today
australien *n.m.* Australian; *adj.* Australian
auto *n.f.* car
autobus *n.m.* bus
autochtone *n.m.* Aboriginal, Native; *adj.*
    Aboriginal, Native
automatique *adj.* automatic
automne *n.m.* fall, autumn
automobile *n.f.* car
autoriser *v.* authorize (to)
autoroute *n.f.* highway
auto-stop (faire de l') *v.* hitchhike (to)
autour de *prep.* around
avaler *v.* swallow (to)
avancé *adj.* advanced
avancer *v.* advance (to)
avant *adv.* before; *prep.* before
avant-dernier *adj.* second from last

avant-midi *n.m.* morning
avec *prep.* with
avertir *v.* warn (to)
aveugle *adj.* blind
avion *n.m.* airplane
aviron *n.m.* rowing
avoir *v.* have (to)
avouer *v.* confess (to); admit (to)

B

bacon *n.m.* bacon
bagnole *n.f. inf.* jalopy
baigner (se) *v.* swim (to)
bail *n.m.* lease (apartment)
bâiller *v.* yawn (to)
bain *n.m.* bath; ~ **à remous** *n.m.* whirlpool;
    ~ **tourbillon** *n.m. qué.* whirlpool
baiser *n.m.* kiss
baisser *v.* lower (to), decrease (to); ~ **(se)**
    v. duck (to)
balayer *v.* sweep (to)
balayeuse *n.f. qué.* vacuum cleaner
balcon *n.m.* balcony
balle *n.f.* ball
ballon *n.m.* ball
banane *n.f.* banana
banque *n.f.* bank
barbu *adj.* bearded
barniques *n.f.pl. qué.* eyeglasses
barque *n.f.* rowboat
barré *adj. qué.* locked
barrer *v. qué.* lock (to); cross out (to)
bas *n.m.* sock; *adj.* low
baseball *n.m.* baseball
basilic *n.m.* basil
basketball *n.m.* basketball
bataille *n.f.* battle; fight

bateau *n.m.* boat
battre *v.* beat (to); ~ **(se)** *v.* fight (to)
bavarder *v.* chat (to)
bazou *n.m. qué. inf.* jalopy
beau *adj.* beautiful
beau-frère *n.m.* brother-in-law
beau-père *n.m.* father-in-law
bébé *n.m.* baby; ~ **la-la** *n.m. qué.* crybaby
bébelle *n.f. qué. inf.* toy
bec *n.m. qué.* kiss
bécosses *n.f.pl. qué. slang* bathroom
beigne *n.m. qué.* doughnut
beignet *n.m.* doughnut
belle-mère *n.f.* mother-in-law
belle-soeur *n.f.* sister-in-law
béluga *n.m.* beluga
bercer *v.* rock (to)
berceuse *n.f. qué.* rocking chair; *n.f.* lullaby
bête puante *n.f. qué.* skunk
bette *n.f. qué.* face
betterave *n.f.* beet
beurre *n.m.* butter; ~ **d'arachides** *n.m.* peanut
butter; ~ **de pinottes** *n.m. qué.* peanut
butter
biathlon *n.m.* biathlon
bibitte *n.f. qué. inf.* bug
bicycle *n.m. qué.* bicycle; ~ **à gaz** *n.m. qué.*
motorcycle
bicyclette *n.f.* bicycle
bidou *n.m. qué. inf.* cash, money
bienvenue *n.f.* welcome
bière *n.f.* beer; ~ **pression** *n.f.* draft beer; ~ **en fût**
n.f. qué. draft beer
billet *n.m.* ticket
binnes *n.f.pl. qué.* baked beans
bitcher *v. qué. slang* complain (to)
blague *n.f.* joke
blâmer *v.* blame (to)
blanc *adj.* white

blé d'Inde *n.m. qué.* corn
blessé *adj.* hurt; injured
blesser *v.* hurt (to)
bleu *adj.* blue
bleuet *n.m.* blueberry
blonde *n.f. qué. inf.* girlfriend
bobettes *n.f.pl. qué. inf.* underwear
boeuf *n.m.* beef; ~ **haché** *n.m.* ground beef
boire *v.* drink (to)
boîte *n.f.* box; ~ **de conserve** *n.f.* can; ~ **de jazz**
  n.f. jazz club; ~ **de nuit** *n.f.* nightclub, disco
bol *n.m.* bowl
bon *adj.* good
botte *n.f.* boot
boucane *n.f. qué.* smoke
bouche *n.f.* mouth
bouder *v.* sulk (to)
boue *n.f.* mud
bouette *n.f. qué. inf.* mud
bouffe *n.f. inf.* food
bouffer *v. inf.* eat (to)
bouger *v.* move (to)
bougie *n.f.* candle
bouillant *adj.* boiling
bouilli *adj.* boiled
bouillir *v.* boil (to)
bouilloire *n.f.* kettle
bourse *n.f.* purse, handbag
boutique *n.f.* shop
brailler *v. qué. inf.* cry (to)
bras *n.m.* arm
brasser *v.* shuffle (to) (playing cards)
brassière *n.f. qué.* bra
briller *v.* shine (to)
brisé *adj.* broken
briser *v.* break (to)
brocoli *n.m.* broccoli
bronzer (se faire) *v.* sunbathe (to)

brosse *n.f.* brush; ~ **à cheveux** *n.f.* hairbrush;
   ~ **à dents** *n.f.* toothbrush
brosser *v.* brush (to)
brûler *v.* burn (to)
brun *adj.* brown
brunante *n.f. qué.* dusk
bruyant *adj.* noisy
buanderie *n.f. qué.* laundromat
bûche de Noël *n.f. qué.* Christmas log, Yule log
bureau de poste *n.m.* post office

C

cabane à sucre *n.f. qué.* sugar shack
cacher *v.* hide (to)
cadeau *n.m.* gift, present
cadran *n.m. qué.* alarm clock
café *n.m.* coffee
calculatrice *n.f.* calculator
calculer *v.* calculate (to)
caleçons *n.m.pl.* underwear
calendrier *n.m.* calendar
caler *v. qué.* sink (to)
calme *adj.* calm
calmer *v.* calm (to)
calorie *n.f.* calorie
calorifère *n.m. qué.* radiator
calotte *n.f. qué. inf.* baseball cap
camp *n.m.* camp; ~ **de vacances** *n.m. qué.*
   summer camp
camper *v.* camp (to)
canadien *n.m.* Canadian; *adj.* Canadian
canadienne *n.f. qué.* parka
canal *n.m. qué.* channel
canapé *n.m.* sofa, couch
canard *n.m.* duck; *n.m. qué.* kettle
canette *n.f. qué.* can
canif *n.m.* pocketknife

canne *n.f. qué.* can; *n.f.* cane
canneberge *n.f.* cranberry
canoë *n.m.* canoe
canot *n.m. qué.* canoe
cantaloup *n.m.* cantaloupe
capable *adj.* able; capable
car *conj.* because; for
carnivore *n.m.* carnivore; *adj.* carnivorous
carotte *n.f.* carrot
carte *n.f.* card; ~ **de crédit** *n.f.* credit card;
   ~ **postale** *n.f.* postcard
casino *n.m.* casino
casquette *n.f.* baseball cap
cassé *adj.* broken
casser *v.* break (to); *v. qué.* break up (to)
   (relationship)
casserole *n.f.* pot
castor *n.m.* beaver
causer *v.* cause (to); chat (to); talk (to)
cave *n.f. qué.* basement
caverne *n.f.* cave
célébrer *v.* celebrate (to)
céleri *n.m.* celery
célibataire *adj.* single
cenne *n.f. qué.* cent
centre *n.m.* center; ~ **commercial** *n.m.* shopping
   center; ~ **d'achat** *n.m. qué.* shopping
   center; ~ **de ski** *n.m.* ski resort
céréales *n.f.pl.* cereal
cerf de Virginie *n.m.* deer
cerise *n.f.* cherry
chaise *n.f.* chair; ~ **berçante** *n.f. qué.* rocking chair
chalet *n.m.* cottage
chaleur *n.f.* heat
chaloupe *n.f.* rowboat
chambre *n.f.* room; ~ **à coucher** *n.f.* bedroom;
   ~ **de bain** *n.f. qué.* bathroom
champignon *n.m.* mushroom
champlure *n.f. qué. inf.* faucet

chandail *n.m.* sweater
chandelle *n.f.* candle
change *n.m. qué.* change (money)
changer *v.* change (to)
chanson *n.f.* song
chanter *v.* sing (to)
chapeau *n.m.* hat
char *n.m. inf.* car
chasse-moustiques *n.m.* bug repellent
chasser *v.* hunt (to); chase (to)
chat *n.m.* cat; ~ **sauvage** *n.m. qué.* raccoon
chaud *adj.* hot; warm; drunk
chaudron *n.m. qué.* pot
chauffer *v.* heat (to)
chauffrette *n.f. qué.* radiator
chaussette *n.f. qué.* slipper; *n.f.* sock
chaussure *n.f.* shoe
chemise *n.f.* shirt; ~ **de nuit** *n.f.* nightgown
chèque *n.m.* check; ~ **de voyage** *n.m.* traveler's
    check
cher *adj.* expensive, pricey; dear
chercher *v.* look for (to)
cheval *n.m.* horse
cheveux *n.m.pl.* hair; **coupe de** ~ *n.f.* haircut
chevreuil *n.m.* deer
chez *prep.* at (somebody's)
chialer *v. qué.* complain (to), whine (to)
chialeux *n.m. qué.* whiner
chicane *n.f. qué.* argument
chicaner (se) *v. qué.* argue (to)
chien *n.m.* dog; ~ **chaud** *n.m.* hot dog
chimie *n.f.* chemistry
chinois *n.m.* Chinese; *adj.* Chinese
chirurgie *n.f.* surgery
chocolat *n.m.* chocolate; **palette de** ~ *n.f. qué.*
    chocolate bar; **tablette de**
    ~ *n.f.* chocolate bar
choisir *v.* choose (to)

chose *n.f.* thing
chou *n.m.* cabbage
chou-fleur *n.m.* cauliflower
chum *n.m. qué. inf.* boyfriend
ciboulette *n.f.* chives
ciel *n.m.* sky
cintre *n.m.* coat hanger
cirque *n.m.* circus
citoyen *n.m.* citizen
citoyenneté *n.f.* citizenship
citron *n.m.* lemon
claque *n.f.* slap, smack; ~s *n.f.pl. qué.* galoshes
clé *n.f.* key
clou *n.m.* nail (hammer)
clouer *v.* nail (to)
cochon *n.m.* pig; ~ d'Inde *n.m.* guinea pig
coffre arrière *n.m.* trunk (of a car)
coïncidence *n.f.* coincidence
collant *adj.* sticky
collation *n.f.* snack
colle *n.f.* glue
coller *v.* glue (to)
collier *n.m.* necklace
côloc *n.m. qué.* roommate
colocataire *n.m.* roommate
colonie de vacances *n.f.* summer camp
combiner *v.* combine (to)
combines *n.f.pl. qué.* long johns
comestible *adj.* edible
commander *v.* command (to); order (to)
commencer *v.* begin (to), start (to)
communiquer *v.* communicate (to)
comparer *v.* compare (to)
complet *n.m.* suit (for men); *adj.* complete
compléter *v.* complete (to)
composer *v.* dial (to); compose (to)
comprendre *v.* understand (to)
compter *v.* count (to)
concevoir *v.* conceive (to)

conclure *v.* conclude (to)

concombre *n.m.* cucumber

conduire *v.* drive (to); lead (to)

confesser *v.* confess (to)

confier *v.* entrust (to); ~ **(se)** *v.* confide (to)

confirmer *v.* confirm (to)

confus *adj.* confused

congédier *v.* fire (to) (employee)

congère *n.f.* snowbank

connaître *v.* know (to)

conseiller *v.* advise (to)

considérer *v.* consider (to)

consoler *v.* console (to)

construire *v.* build (to)

consulat *n.m.* consulate

consulter *v.* consult (to)

contenir *v.* contain (to)

continuer *v.* continue (to)

contre *prep.* against

contribuer *v.* contribute (to)

convaincre *v.* convince (to)

coopérer *v.* cooperate (to)

copain *n.m.* boyfriend

copier *v.* copy (to)

copine *n.f.* girlfriend

corde *n.f.* rope

cossin *n.m. qué. inf.* thing

costarde *n.f. qué.* custard

costume de bain *n.m. qué.* bathing suit, swimsuit

cou *n.m.* neck

coucher *v.* put to bed (to); lay down (to); ~ **(se)**
    v. go to bed (to); lie down (to)

coudre *v.* sew (to); stitch (to)

couette *n.f.* duvet, comforter

couler *v.* sink (to) (boat)

coupe *n.f.* wine glass; ~ **de vin** glass of wine

couper *v.* cut (to)

courge *n.f.* squash (vegetable)

courgette *n.f.* zucchini

courir *v.* run (to)
courriel *n.m. qué.* e-mail
courrier *n.m.* mail
court *adj.* short
cousin *n.m.* cousin
couteau *n.m.* knife
coutellerie *n.f.* cutlery
coûter *v.* cost (to)
coûteux *adj.* expensive
couvert *adj.* covered
couverte *n.f. qué.* blanket
couverture *n.f.* blanket
couvrir *v.* cover (to)
cracher *v.* spit (to)
craindre *v.* fear (to)
craire *v. qué. inf.* believe (to)
crayon *n.m.* pencil
créatif *adj.* creative
créer *v.* create (to)
crémage *n.m. qué.* icing
crème *n.f.* cream; ~ **à mains** *n.f.* hand cream;
    ~ **glacée** *n.f.* ice cream; ~ **solaire** *n.f.*
    sunscreen
crémeux *adj.* creamy
crêpe *n.f.* crepe, pancake
crépuscule *n.m.* dusk
creuser *v.* dig (to)
crevette *n.f.* shrimp
crier *v.* yell (to)
critiquer *v.* complain (to)
croire *v.* believe (to)
cru *adj.* raw
cuillère *n.f.* spoon; ~ **à soupe** *n.f.* tablespoon;
    ~ **à table** *n.f. qué.* tablespoon; ~ **à thé** *n.f.*
    qué. teaspoon
cuire *v.* cook (to)
cuisiner *v.* cook (to)
cuit *adj.* cooked

cultiver *v.* cultivate (to)
curling *n.m.* curling
cyclisme *n.m.* cycling

D

dans *prep.* in
danser *v.* dance (to)
date *n.f.* date (day)
datte *n.f.* date (fruit)
de *prep.* about; from; of
débarbouillette *n.f. qué.* washcloth, facecloth
débarquer *v.* get off (to)
débarré *adj. qué.* unlocked
débarrer *v. qué.* unlock (to)
débattre *v.* debate (to)
déborder *v.* overflow (to)
déchet *n.m.* garbage
déchirer *v.* tear (to)
décider *v.* decide (to)
déclarer *v.* declare (to)
décoller *v.* take off (to) (airplane)
décorer *v.* decorate (to)
décourager *v.* discourage (to)
découvrir *v.* discover (to)
décrire *v.* describe (to)
déçu *adj.* disappointed
défaire *v.* undo (to)
défendre *v.* defend (to); forbid (to)
dégoûtant *adj.* disgusting
déguédiner (se) *v. qué.* hurry up (to)
dégueulasse *adj. inf.* disgusting
dégueuler *v. qué. slang* vomit (to)
déguiser *v.* disguise (to)
déjeuner *n.m. qué.* breakfast; **petit ~** *n.m.*
    breakfast
demander *v.* ask (to)
déménager *v.* move (to) (residence)

demeurer *v.* stay (to)

démolir *v.* demolish (to)

dentaire *adj.* dental

dentifrice *n.m.* toothpaste

dépanneur *n.m. qué.* general store, convenience store

dépasser *v.* pass (to) (car)

dépêcher (se) *v.* hurry up (to)

dépendre *v.* depend (to)

dépenser *v.* spend (to) (money)

déposer *v.* deposit (to)

depuis *prep.* since

dernier *adj.* last

derrière *prep.* behind

descendre *v.* go down (to); descend (to)

désespérer *v.* despair (to)

déshabiller *v.* undress (to); ~ **(se)** *v.* undress (to) (oneself)

désirer *v.* wish (to); desire (to)

désobéir *v.* disobey (to)

dessiner *v.* draw (to)

détacher *v.* detach (to)

déterminer *v.* determine (to)

détester *v.* detest (to), hate (to)

détruire *v.* destroy (to)

deuxième *adj.* second

devant *n.m.* front; *prep.* in front of

développer *v.* develop (to)

devenir *v.* become (to)

déverrouillé *adj.* unlocked

déverrouiller *v.* unlock (to)

deviner *v.* guess (to)

devoir *v.* owe (to)

dévorer *v.* devour (to)

diamant *n.m.* diamond

dictionnaire *n.m.* dictionary

difficile *adj.* difficult

diminuer *v.* decrease (to), diminish (to)

dinde *n.f.* turkey

dîner *n.m. qué.* lunch
dire *v.* tell (to); say (to)
diriger *v.* direct (to); supervise (to); lead (to);
    conduct (to) (orchestra)
discothèque *n.f.* disco, nightclub
discuter *v.* discuss (to)
disparaître *v.* disappear (to)
dispendieux *adj.* expensive
distinguer *v.* distinguish (to)
distribuer *v.* distribute (to)
divan *n.m.* sofa, couch
diviser *v.* divide (to)
divorcé *adj.* divorced
doigt *n.m.* finger
donc *conj.* so
donner *v.* give (to)
dormir *v.* sleep (to)
dos *n.m.* back
doubler *v.* double (to)
douche *n.f.* shower
douillette *n.f. qué.* duvet
douter *v.* doubt (to)
doux *adj.* soft; gentle
draff *n.f. qué. inf.* draft beer
drète *adv. qué. slang* straight
droit *n.m.* law; *adj.* straight; *adv.* straight
droite *n.f.* right (direction)
drôle *adj.* funny
dull *adj. qué. slang.* dull
durant *prep.* during
durer *v.* last (to)
duvet *n.m.* duvet

E

eau *n.f.* water; ~ **de source** *n.f.* spring water
écarter (s') *v. qué.* get lost (to)
échanger *v.* exchange (to)

échapper *v.* drop (to)
écharpe *n.f.* scarf
échouer *v.* fail (to)
école *n.f.* school
économie *n.f.* economy
économiser *v.* save (to) (time, money)
écouter *v.* listen (to)
écran *n.m.* screen; ~ **solaire** *n.m.* sunscreen
écrapoutir *v. qué. slang* crush (to)
écraser *v.* crush (to); flatten (to)
écrire *v.* write (to)
écrit *adj.* written
écureuil *n.m.* squirrel
effacer *v.* erase (to); delete (to)
effectuer *v.* carry out (to), accomplish (to)
efficace *adj.* effective, efficient
effoirer *v. qué. slang* flatten (to); ~ **(s')** *v.* sprawl
    out (to)
effrayé *adj.* scared
égocentrique *adj.* egocentric
égoïste *adj.* selfish, egotistical
élaboré *adj.* elaborate
électricité *n.f.* electricity
électrique *adj.* electrical, electric
électronique *adj.* electronic
élire *v.* elect (to)
emballer *v.* wrap (to)
embarquer *v.* get on (to)
embaucher *v.* hire (to)
embrasser *v.* kiss (to)
émigrer *v.* emigrate (to)
employer *v.* employ (to); use (to)
emprunter *v.* borrow (to)
en *prep.* in; on; to; ~ **face de** *prep.* across from
encourager *v.* encourage (to)
énervé *adj.* agitated
enfant *n.m.* child
enfuir **(s')** *v.* flee (to), run away (to)
engagé *adj. qué.* busy (telephone line)

engager *v.* hire (to)
engraisser *v.* gain weight (to)
enlever *v.* remove (to), take off (to)
ennuyant *adj.* boring, dull
ennuyer *v.* bore (to); annoy (to)
ennuyeux *adj.* boring, dull
enquêter *v.* investigate (to)
enregistrer *v.* register (to); record (to)
enseigner *v.* teach (to)
ensoleillé *adj.* sunny
ensuite *conj.* next
entendre *v.* hear (to)
enterrer *v.* bury (to)
entêté *adj.* stubborn
entourer *v.* surround (to)
entracte *n.f.* intermission
entraîner *v.* train (to)
entre *prep.* between
entrer *v.* enter (to)
entrevoir *v.* glimpse (to)
entrouvert *adj.* ajar
envahir *v.* invade (to)
envaler *v. qué.* swallow (to)
enveloppe *n.f.* envelope
envelopper *v.* envelop (to), wrap (to)
envié *adj.* envied
environ *prep.* approximately
envoyer *v.* send (to)
épais *adj.* thick; *adj. qué.* dumb
épargner *v.* save (to) (money)
épice *n.f.* spice
épicé *adj.* spicy
épinard *n.m.* spinach
épluchette *n.f. qué.* corn roast; ~ **de blé d'Inde**
        n.f. qué. corn roast
épouser *v.* wed (to), marry (to)
épuiser *v.* exhaust (to), use up (to)
équilibre *n.m.* balance

erreur *n.f.* mistake
escargot *n.m.* snail
escrime *n.m.* fencing
espagnol *n.m.* Spanish; *adj.* Spanish
espérer *v.* wish (to); hope (to)
essayer *v.* try (to); try on (to)
essence *n.f.* gas
essuyer *v.* dry (to); wipe (to)
est *n.m.* east
estimer *v.* estimate (to)
et *conj.* and
établir *v.* establish (to)
étage *n.m.* floor
étaler (s') *v.* sprawl out (to)
États-Unis *n.m.pl.* United States
été *n.m.* summer; ~ des Indiens *n.m.* Indian
        Summer; ~ indien *n.m. qué.* Indian
        Summer
éteindre *v.* extinguish (to), put out (to) (fire)
étendre *v.* lay down (to); ~ (s') *v.* lie down (to)
étoile *n.f.* star
étrange *adj.* strange
être *v.* be (to)
étudiant *n.m.* student
étudier *v.* study (to)
européen *n.m.* European; *adj.* European
évanouir (s') *v.* faint (to)
éveiller *v.* wake (to); ~ (s') wake (to) (oneself)
évier *n.m.* sink (kitchen)
éviter *v.* avoid (to)
exagérer *v.* exaggerate (to)
examiner *v.* examine (to)
excellent *adj.* excellent
excepté *prep.* except
excitant *adj.* exciting
excuser *v.* excuse (to)
exiger *v.* demand (to); require (to)
exister *v.* exist (to)

expliquer *v.* explain (to)
exporter *v.* export (to)

F

fabriquer *v.* manufacture (to); make (to)
face *n.f.* face
facile *adj.* easy
facture *n.f.* bill
faire *v.* do (to); make (to)
famille *n.f.* family
fatigué *adj.* tired
fausser *v.* sing off-key (to)
faux *adj.* false
féliciter *v.* congratulate (to)
fenêtre *n.f.* window
fer *n.m.* iron (metal); ~ **à repasser** *n.m.* iron
    (appliance)
ferme *n.f.* farm; *adj.* firm
fermé *adj.* closed
fermer *v.* close (to)
fermeture éclair *n.f.* zipper
fermoir *n.m.* zipper
feu *n.m.* fire; ~ **de camp** *n.m.* campfire;
    ~ **de circulation** *n.m.* traffic light
fève *n.f.* bean; ~s **au lard** *n.f.pl. qué.* baked
    beans *pl.*
fiancé *n.m.* fiancé; *adj.* engaged
fier *adj.* proud
figue *n.f.* fig
fille *n.f.* girl; daughter
film *n.m.* movie
fils *n.m.* son
fin *n.f.* end; *adj. qué.* nice, kind; ~ **de semaine**
    n.f. weekend
finir *v.* finish (to), end (to)
flanc-mou *adj. qué.* lazy
flash *n.m. qué.* idea

fleur *n.f.* flower
fleuriste *n.m.* florist
flo *n.m. qué. inf.* child
flotter *v.* float (to)
fluctuer *v.* fluctuate (to)
flyer *v. qué. slang* speed (to)
fondant au chocolat *n.m.* fudge
fondre *v.* melt (to)
fontaine *n.f.* water fountain
football *n.m.* American football
forcer *v.* force (to)
forger *v.* forge (to)
former *v.* form (to)
fort *adj.* strong
fou *adj.* crazy
foulard *n.m.* scarf
four *n.m.* oven
fourchette *n.f.* fork
fourgonnette *n.f.* van
fournaise *n.f.* furnace
fournir *v.* supply (to), provide (to)
foyer *n.m.* fireplace
frais *adj.* fresh; cool; *adj. qué.* snobby, pretentious
fraise *n.f.* strawberry
framboise *n.f.* raspberry
français *n.m.* French; *adj.* French
frapper *v.* hit (to)
fréquent *adj.* frequent
fréquenter *v.* associate with (to); date (to)
frère *n.m.* brother
frette *adj. qué. slang* cold
frigidaire *n.m. qué.* refrigerator
frit *adj.* fried
frite *n.f.* French fry
froid *n.m.* cold (temperature); *adj.* cold
fromage *n.m.* cheese
frotter *v.* rub (to)
fructueux *adj.* fruitful

fruit *n.m.* fruit; ~ **de la passion** *n.m.* passion
fruit; ~ **de mer** *n.m.* seafood
fudge *n.m. qué.* fudge
fuir *v.* flee (to), run away (to)
fumée *n.f.* smoke
fumer *v.* smoke (to)

G

gager *v. qué.* bet (to)
gagner *v.* win (to)
galerie *n.f. qué.* balcony; *n.f.* gallery
garantir *v.* guarantee (to)
garçon *n.m.* boy
garder *v.* babysit (to); keep (to)
gare *n.f.* train station
garrocher *v. qué. slang* throw (to)
gâteau *n.m.* cake
gauche *n.f.* left (direction)
gaufre *n.f.* waffle
gaz *n.m. qué.* gas
gazeux *adj.* carbonated
gelé *adj.* frozen
geler *v.* freeze (to)
gênant *adj.* bothersome; embarrassing
gêné *adj.* embarrassed; timid
gêner *v.* bother (to); embarrass (to)
génie *n.m.* engineering
gentil *adj.* nice
géographie *n.f.* geography
géologie *n.f.* geology
glaçage *n.m.* icing
glissade d'eau *n.f.* water slide
glisser *v.* slide (to)
glissoire *n.f.* slide
global *adj.* global
glouton *adj.* gluttonous
gonfler *v.* inflate (to)

gougounes *n.f.pl. qué.* flip-flops
gourde *n.f.* canteen; squash (vegetable)
gourmand *adj.* gluttonous
goûter *v.* taste (to)
grand *adj.* tall
grandir *v.* grow (to), grow up (to)
grand-mère *n.f.* grandmother
grand-père *n.m.* grandfather
gras *n.m.* fat; *adj.* fat
gratte-ciel *n.m.* skyscraper
gratter *v.* scratch (to)
grec *n.m.* Greek; *adj.* Greek
grelotter *v.* shiver (to)
grignoter *v.* snack (to)
griller (se faire) *v. qué.* sunbathe (to)
grimper *v.* climb (to)
gris *adj.* gray
grogner *v.* growl (to); grunt (to)
gros *adj.* fat, big
guénille *n.f. qué. inf.* rag
guérir *v.* cure (to), heal (to); recover (to) (illness)
gueule de bois *n.f.* hangover
gugusse *n.f. qué. inf.* thing
guichet automatique *n.m.* ATM, bank machine
guide *n.m.* guide
guider *v.* guide (to)
gymnastique *n.f.* gymnastics *pl.*

H

habillé *adj.* dressed
habiller *v.* dress (to); ~ (s') dress (to) (oneself)
habiter *v.* live in (to)
haï *adj.* hated
haïr *v.* hate (to)
handicapé *adj.* disabled
haricot *n.m.* bean

hausser *v.* increase (to), raise (to)
haut *adj.* high
hebdomadaire *adj.* weekly
hériter *v.* inherit (to)
hésiter *v.* hesitate (to)
heure *n.f.* hour
heureux *adj.* happy
hibou *n.m.* owl
histoire *n.f.* history; story
hiver *n.m.* winter
hockey *n.m.* hockey
hollandais *n.m.* Dutch; *adj.* Dutch
hôpital *n.m.* hospital
horrible *adj.* horrible
hot-dog *n.m.* hot dog
hôtel *n.m.* hotel
huard *n.m.* loon
huile *n.f.* oil
huileux *adj.* oily
humilier *v.* humiliate (to)
hygiénique *adj.* hygienic

I

ici *adv.* here
icitte *adv. qué. slang* here
idée *n.f.* idea
idiot *n.m.* idiot
ignorant *adj.* ignorant
ignorer *v.* ignore (to)
illuminer *v.* illuminate (to)
illustré *adj.* illustrated
imaginer *v.* imagine (to)
imbécile *adj.* imbecile
imiter *v.* imitate (to)
immangeable *adj.* inedible
immédiat *adj.* immediate

immigrer *v.* immigrate (to)
impeccable *adj.* impeccable, flawless
impératif *adj.* imperative
importer *v.* import (to)
imposer *v.* impose (to)
imprimer *v.* print (to)
improviser *v.* improvise (to)
inclure *v.* include (to)
indiquer *v.* indicate (to)
inévitable *adj.* inevitable
infirmière *n.f.* nurse
informer *v.* inform (to)
inimaginable *adj.* unimaginable
inondation *n.f.* flood
inonder *v.* flood (to)
inquiet *adj.* worried, concerned
insecte *n.m.* bug, insect
inspirer *v.* inspire (to)
installer *v.* install (to)
instruire *v.* instruct (to); teach (to)
insultant *adj.* insulting
insulté *adj.* insulted
intelligent *adj.* intelligent
interdire *v.* prohibit (to), forbid (to)
intéressant *adj.* interesting
intermission *n.f. qué.* intermission
interroger *v.* interrogate (to)
interrompre *v.* interrupt (to)
interrupteur *n.m.* switch
intersection *n.f.* intersection
introduire *v.* introduce (to)
inventer *v.* invent (to)
invitant *adj.* inviting
inviter *v.* invite (to)
irriter *v.* irritate (to)
isoler *v.* isolate (to)
italien *n.m.* Italian; *adj.* Italian
ivre *adj.* drunk

J

jamais *adv.* never
jambe *n.f.* leg
jambon *n.m.* ham
japonais *n.m.* Japanese; *adj.* Japanese
jaquette *n.f. qué.* nightgown
jardin *n.m.* garden
jaser *v. qué.* chat (to)
jaune *adj.* yellow
jeter *v.* throw away (to)
jeune *adj.* young
job *n.f. qué.* work, job
joindre *v.* join (to), unite (to)
joke *n.f. qué.* joke
jouer *v.* play (to)
jouet *n.m.* toy
jour *n.m.* day
journée *n.f.* day
joyeux *adj.* merry, cheerful
jupe *n.f.* skirt
jurer *v.* swear (to)
jus *n.m.* juice
jusqu'à *prep.* until
juteux *adj.* juicy

K

kayak *n.m.* kayak
kilométrage *n.m.* mileage
kitsch *adj.* kitsch
kiwi *n.m.* kiwi

L

lâcher *v.* let go (to)
laid *adj.* ugly

laisser *v.* leave (to)
lait *n.m.* milk
laitue *n.f.* lettuce
lampe *n.f.* lamp; ~ **de poche** *n.f.* flashlight
lancer *v.* throw (to); pitch (to)
langue *n.f.* tongue; language
lapin *n.m.* rabbit
lavabo *n.m.* sink (bathroom)
laver *v.* wash (to)
lècher *v.* lick (to)
léger *adj.* light
lent *adj.* slow
lettre *n.f.* letter
lever *v.* lift (to); raise (to)
licher *v. qué.* lick (to)
lilas *n.m.* lilac; *adj.* lilac
lime *n.f.* lime
limité *adj.* limited
liqueur *n.f. qué.* soda; *n.f.* liqueur
liquide *n.m.* liquid; *adj.* liquid
lire *v.* read (to)
lit *n.m.* bed
littérature *n.f.* literature
livre *n.m.* book
livrer *v.* deliver (to)
loi *n.f.* law
loin *adj.* far; ~ **de** *prep.* far from
long *adj.* long
loué *adj.* rented, leased
louer *v.* rent (to), lease (to)
loup *n.m.* wolf
lourd *adj.* heavy
lu *adj.* read
luciole *n.f.* firefly
luire *v.* glow (to), shine (to)
luisant *adj.* shiny
lumière *n.f.* light; *n.f. qué.* traffic light
lunch *n.m.* lunch
lune *n.f.* moon

lunettes *n.f.pl.* eyeglasses
lutte *n.f.* wrestling; struggle
luxueux *adj.* luxurious

M

mâcher *v.* chew (to)
magané *adj. qué. slang* used
magasin *n.m.* store
magasinage *n.m. qué.* shopping
magasiner *v. qué.* shop (to)
magnétoscope *n.m.* VCR
maigre *adj.* lean; skinny
maigrir *v.* lose weight (to)
maillot de bain *n.m.* bathing suit, swimsuit
main *n.f.* hand
maintenant *adv.* now
maintenir *v.* maintain (to)
mais *conj.* but
maïs *n.m.* corn
maison *n.f.* house
maîtriser *v.* master (to)
malade *adj.* sick; *adj. qué.* crazy
malheureux *adj.* unhappy
malle *n.f. qué.* mail
manger *n.m.* food; *v.* eat (to)
mangue *n.f.* mango
manquer *v.* miss (to); lack (to)
manteau *n.m.* coat
manuel *n.m.* manual; *adj.* manual
marche *n.f.* walk
marcher *v.* walk (to)
marié *adj.* married
marier *v.* marry (to), wed (to)
maringouin *n.m.* mosquito
marketing *n.m.* marketing
marmotte *n.f.* woodchuck
marquer *v.* mark (to)

marron *n.m.* chestnut; *adj.* brown
matante *n.f. qué. inf.* aunt
mathématiques *n.f.pl.* mathematics *pl.*
matin *n.m.* morning
mauvais *adj.* bad
mauve *adj.* purple
méchant *adj.* mean
médecin *n.m.* doctor
médecine *n.f.* medecine
médical *adj.* medical
meilleur *n.m.* best; *adj.* better
mélancolique *adj.* melancoly
mélanger *v.* mix (to); blend (to)
mêlé *adj. qué.* confused
mélodie *n.f.* melody
melon d'eau *n.m. qué.* watermelon
mendier *v.* beg (to) (for money)
mensuel *adj.* monthly
mentir *v.* lie (to)
mère *n.f.* mother
mériter *v.* deserve (to)
merveilleux *adj.* wonderful
mesure *n.f.* measure
mesurer *v.* measure (to)
mettre *v.* put (to)
micro-ondes *n.m.* microwave
midi *n.m.* noon
millage *n.m.* mileage
mince *adj.* thin
minoune *n.f. qué. inf.* jalopy
minute *n.f.* minute
miroir *n.m.* mirror
mitaine *n.f.* mitt, mitten
moderne *adj.* modern
moindre *adj.* least
monnaie *n.f.* change (money)
mononcle *n.m. qué. inf.* uncle
monter *v.* go up (to); climb (to), ascend (to);
    get on (to) (bike, horse)

montre *n.f.* watch
montrer *v.* show (to)
morceau *n.m.* piece
mordre *v.* bite (to)
mort *adj.* dead
motocyclette *n.f.* motorcycle
mouche *n.f.* fly; ~ **à feu** *n.f. qué.* firefly
mouchoir *n.m.* tissue
mouffette *n.f.* skunk
mouiller *v.* wet (to); moisten (to); dampen (to);
    soak (to); *qué.* rain (to)
mourir *v.* die (to)
moustique *n.m.* bug, insect
mouton *n.m.* sheep
moyen *adj.* average; medium
moyenne *n.f.* average
muet *adj.* mute
multiple *adj.* multiple
multiplier *v.* multiply (to)
mur *n.m.* wall
musée *n.m.* museum
musical *adj.* musical
musique *n.f.* music

N

nager *v.* swim (to)
naître *v.* born (to be)
natation *n.f.* swimming
nationalité *n.f.* nationality
navet *n.m.* turnip
nectarine *n.f.* nectarine
négliger *v.* neglect (to); disregard (to)
neige *n.f.* snow; **banc de** ~ *n.m. qué.* snowbank
neiger *v.* snow (to)
nerveux *adj.* nervous
nettoyer *v.* clean (to)
nettoyeur *n.m. qué.* dry cleaner

neuf *adj.* new
nez *n.m.* nose
ni *conj.* neither, nor
niais *adj.* idiot
niaiseux *n.m. qué.* idiot
nier *v.* deny (to)
noir *adj.* black
noirceur *n.f. qué.* darkness
nom *n.m.* name
nommer *v.* name (to)
non *adv.* no
nono *n.m. qué. slang* idiot
nord *n.m.* north
nord-américain *n.m.* North American;
　　adj. North American
note *n.f.* note
noter *v.* note (to)
nourrir *v.* feed (to); ~ **(se)** feed (to) (oneself)
nourriture *n.f.* food
nouveau *adj.* new
nu *adj.* naked
nuage *n.m.* cloud
nuageux *adj.* cloudy
nuit *n.f.* night

O

obéir *v.* obey (to)
obéissant *adj.* obedient
obliger *v.* oblige (to)
observer *v.* observe (to)
obtenir *v.* obtain (to)
occidental *adj.* western
occupé *adj.* busy
occuper *v.* occupy (to); ~ **(s')** take care of (to)
oeil *n.m.* eye
oeuf *n.m.* egg
offenser *v.* offend (to)

officiel *adj.* official
officieux *adj.* unofficial
offrir *v.* offer (to)
oie *n.f.* goose
oignon *n.m.* onion
oiseau *n.m.* bird
omelette *n.f.* omelet
oncle *n.m.* uncle
ongle *n.m.* nail (finger/toe)
opérer *v.* operate (to)
opposer *v.* oppose (to)
or *n.m.* gold; *adj.* gold
orage *n.m.* thunderstorm
orange *n.f.* orange; *adj.* orange
orchestre *n.m.* orchestra
ordinateur *n.m.* computer
ordonnance *n.f.* prescription
ordure *n.f.* garbage
oreille *n.f.* ear; **boucle d'~** *n.f.* earring
oreiller *n.m.* pillow; **taie d'~** *n.f.* pillowcase
organiser *v.* organize (to)
oriental *adj.* eastern; oriental; Asian
origan *n.m.* oregano
orignal *n.m.* moose
orteil *n.m.* toe
oser *v.* dare (to)
ôter *v.* take away (to); take off (to), remove (to)
ou *conj.* or
où *adv.* where; *conj.* where
ouaouaron *n.m. qué.* bullfrog
oublier *v.* forget (to)
ouest *n.m.* west
oui *adv.* yes
ours *n.m.* bear
outarde *n.f. qué.* Canada goose
ouvert *adj.* open
ouvre-boîte *n.m.* can opener
ouvrir *v.* open (to)

P

pain *n.m.* bread
pâle *adj.* pale; light
pamplemousse *n.m.* grapefruit
panais *n.m.* parsnip
pantalon *n.m.* pants *pl.*
pantoufle *n.f.* slipper
papaye *n.f.* papaya
papier *n.m.* paper
paqueté *adj. qué. slang* drunk
par *prep.* by
paraître *v.* appear (to); seem (to)
parc *n.m.* park
parcomètre *n.m.* parking meter
pardonner *v.* forgive (to)
paresseux *adj.* lazy
parfum *n.m.* perfume
parfumer *v.* perfume (to)
pari *n.m.* bet
parier *v.* bet (to)
parka *n.f.* parka
parlé *adj.* spoken
parler *v.* talk (to)
parmi *prep.* among
partager *v.* share (to)
partir *v.* leave (to)
passeport *n.m.* passport
passer *v.* pass (to)
passif *adj.* passive
pastèque *n.f.* watermelon
pastille *n.f.* throat lozenge
patate *n.f. qué.* potato; ~ frite *n.f. qué.* French fry
pâté chinois *n.m.* shepherd's pie
patente *n.f. qué. inf.* thing
pâtes *n.f.pl.* pasta
patin *n.m.* skate
patinage *n.m.* skating; ~ artistique *n.m.* figure
skating; ~ de vitesse *n.m.* speed skating

patiner *v.* skate (to)
patio *n.m. qué.* patio, deck
pauvre *adj.* poor
payer *v.* pay (to)
pêche *n.f.* peach; fishing
pêcher *v.* fish (to)
peigne *n.m.* comb
peigner *v.* comb (to)
peignoir *n.m.* robe
peindre *v.* paint (to)
peinturer *v. qué.* paint (to)
peler *v.* peel (to)
pencher *v.* tilt (to); incline (to); ~ **(se)** *v.* bend
     over (to)
pendant *prep.* during, while
penser *v.* think (to)
perdre *v.* lose (to); ~ **(se)** get lost (to)
perdu *adj.* lost
père *n.m.* father
permettre *v.* permit (to), allow (to)
persil *n.m.* parsley
persuader *v.* persuade (to)
pesant *adj.* heavy
peser *v.* weigh (to)
pété *adj. qué. inf.* broken
péter *v. qué. inf.* break (to)
petit *adj.* short; little; small
peur *n.f.* fear; **avoir** ~ *v.* fear (to)
pharmaceutique *adj.* pharmaceutical
physique *n.f.* physics; *adj.* physical
piasse *n.f. qué. inf.* buck (money)
piastre *n.f. qué. inf.* buck (money)
pièce *n.f.* coin; room
pied *n.m.* foot
pilote *n.m.* pilot
piloter *v.* pilot (to)
piment *n.m. qué.* pepper (vegetable)
pincer *v.* pinch (to)
piquant *adj.* spicy

piquer *v.* sting (to); *v. inf.* steal (to)
piscine *n.f.* pool
pitcher *v. qué. slang* pitch (to)
placer *v.* place (to)
placoter *v. qué.* chat (to)
plafond *n.m.* ceiling
plage *n.f.* beach
plaindre (se) *v.* complain (to)
plaire *v.* please (to)
plan *n.m.* plan
planche à neige *n.f.* snowboard
plancher *n.m.* floor
planifier *v.* plan (to)
plante *n.f.* plant
planter *v.* plant (to); *qué. slang* beat (to) (someone)
plate *adj. qué.* boring
plausible *adj.* plausible
plein *adj.* full
plemer *v. qué.* peel (to) (skin)
pleurer *v.* cry (to)
pleuvoir *v.* rain (to)
plier *v.* bend (to)
plonger *v.* dive (to)
pluie *n.f.* rain
pluvieux *adj.* rainy
poche *n.f.* pocket
poêlon *n.m.* pan
poêlonne *n.f. qué.* pan
poids *n.m.* weight
poire *n.f.* pear
pois *n.m.* pea; ~ **chiche** *n.m.* chickpea;
    ~ **mange-tout** *n.m.* snowpea
poisson *n.m.* fish
poivre *n.m.* pepper (spice)
poivron *n.m.* pepper (vegetable)
polir *v.* polish (to)
pomme *n.f.* apple; ~ **de terre** *n.f.* potato
populaire *adj.* popular
poque *n.f. qué. slang* hockey puck, puck

porc *n.m.* pork
porte *n.f.* door
portefeuille *n.m.* wallet
porter *v.* carry (to); wear (to) (clothes)
portugais *n.m.* Portuguese; *adj.* Portuguese
posséder *v.* own (to); possess (to)
poteau *n.m.* post, pole
pouce *n.m.* thumb; **faire du** ~ *v. qué.* hitchhike (to)
poulet *n.m.* chicken
pour *prep.* for
pourquoi *adv.* why; *conj.* why
pourrir *v.* rot (to)
poursuivre *v.* pursue (to); sue (to)
pousser *v.* push (to)
poutine *n.f. qué.* poutine
pouvoir *n.m.* power; *v.* able (to be)
pratique *adj.* practical
pratiquer *v.* practice (to)
précédent *adj.* previous
précéder *v.* precede (to)
précis *adj.* precise
préféré *adj.* favorite
préférer *v.* prefer (to)
premier *adj.* first
prendre *v.* take (to)
préparer *v.* prepare (to)
près *adj.* near; *adv.* close; ~ **de** *prep.* close to
prescription *n.f. qué.* prescription
présenter *v.* present (to); introduce (to)
prétendre *v.* pretend (to)
prétentieux *adj.* pretentious
prêter *v.* lend (to)
prévenir *v.* prevent (to); warn (to)
prévoir *v.* forecast (to), foresee (to)
printemps *n.m.* spring (season)
privé *adj.* private
priver *v.* deprive (to)
prix *n.m.* price
prochain *adj.* next

procurer (se) *v.* get (to)
produire *v.* produce (to)
projet *n.m.* project
promesse *n.f.* promise
promettre *v.* promise (to)
proposer *v.* propose (to)
propre *adj.* clean
protéger *v.* protect (to)
protester *v.* protest (to)
prouver *v.* prove (to)
provoquer *v.* provoke (to)
prune *n.f.* plum
psychologie *n.f.* psychology
public *adj.* public
publier *v.* publish (to)
puis *conj.* then
punir *v.* punish (to)

Q

quand *adv.* when; *conj.* when
québécois *n.m.* Québécois, Quebecer; *adj.*
        Québécois, Quebecer
question *n.f.* question
questionner *v.* question (to)
quétaine *adj. qué.* cheesy, tacky, kitsch
qui *pron.* who
quitter *v.* leave (to)
quoi *pron.* what
quotidien *adj.* daily

R

raconter *v.* tell (to)
radiateur *n.m.* radiator
radio *n.f.* radio
radis *n.m.* radish

raisin *n.m.* grape
ramener *v.* bring back (to)
ramer *v.* row (to)
ramper *v.* crawl (to)
rapide *adj.* fast
rapporter *v.* bring back (to)
rapprocher *v.* bring closer (to)
raquette *n.f.* raquet; ~s *n.f.pl. qué.* snowshoes
rare *adj.* rare
rarement *adv.* rarely, seldom
rasoir *n.m.* razor
rassurer *v.* reassure (to)
raton laveur *n.m.* raccoon
rayé *adj.* striped
réaliser *v.* realize (to)
récent *adj.* recent
recette *n.f.* recipe
recevoir *v.* receive (to)
rechercher *v.* research (to)
réciter *v.* recite (to)
recommandé *adj.* recommended
recommander *v.* recommend (to)
reconnaître *v.* recognize (to)
reculer *v.* back up (to)
redire *v.* tell again (to), say again (to)
redonner *v.* give back (to)
réduire *v.* diminish (to), decrease (to), reduce (to)
refaire *v.* redo (to)
réfléchir *v.* think over (to)
réfrigérateur *n.m.* refrigerator
refroidir *v.* chill (to), cool (to)
refuser *v.* refuse (to)
regarder *v.* look (to), watch (to)
regretter *v.* regret (to)
rejeter *v.* reject (to)
remarquer *v.* notice (to); note (to); observe (to)
rembourser *v.* reimburse (to)
remercier *v.* thank (to)
remettre *v.* put back (to); give back (to)

remonte-pente *n.m.* T-bar, chairlift
remplacer *v.* replace (to)
remplir *v.* fill (to)
renard *n.m.* fox
rencontrer *v.* meet (to)
rendez-vous *n.m.* date; appointment
rendre *v.* give back (to)
renseigner *v.* inform (to)
renvoyer *v.* send back (to)
réparer *v.* repair (to), fix (to)
repas *n.m.* meal
repasser *v.* iron (to)
répéter *v.* repeat (to)
répondre *v.* answer (to)
réponse *n.f.* answer
reposer *v.* rest (to); ~ **(se)** rest (to) (oneself)
représenter *v.* represent (to)
reprocher *v.* reproach (to)
réserver *v.* reserve (to)
résider *v.* reside (to)
résister *v.* resist (to)
résoudre *v.* solve (to); resolve (to)
respecter *v.* respect (to)
respirer *v.* breathe (to)
ressentir *v.* feel (to)
restaurant *n.m.* restaurant
rester *v.* stay (to)
résultat *n.m.* result
résulter *v.* result (to)
retourner *v.* go back (to)
retraité *adj.* retired
retrouver *v.* recover (to), find again (to)
réunir *v.* reunite (to)
réussir *v.* succeed (to)
réveiller *v.* wake (to); ~ **(se)** wake (to) (oneself)
réveil-matin *n.m.* alarm clock
révéler *v.* reveal (to)
revenir *v.* come back (to)

rêver *v.* dream (to)
réviser *v.* revise (to)
revoir *v.* see again (to)
rez-de-chaussée *n.m.* first floor
rhume *n.m.* cold (illness)
riche *adj.* rich
ride *n.f.* wrinkle
ridé *adj.* wrinkled
ridicule *adj.* ridiculous
ridiculiser *v.* ridicule (to)
rimer *v.* rhyme (to)
rire *v.* laugh (to)
risquer *v.* risk (to)
robe *n.f.* dress; ~ **de chambre** *n.f. qué.* robe
robinet *n.m.* faucet
roche *n.f.* rock
romarin *n.m.* rosemary
rompre *v.* break up (to) (relationship)
rondelle *n.f.* hockey puck, puck
ronfler *v.* snore (to)
rose *n.f.* rose; *adj.* pink
rôti *n.m.* roast; *adj.* roasted
rôtie *n.f.* toast
rôtir *v.* roast (to)
rouge *adj.* red
rougir *v.* blush (to)
rouler *v.* roll (to)
rue *n.f.* street
ruiner *v.* ruin (to)
russe *n.m.* Russian; *adj.* Russian

S

sable *n.m.* sand
sac *n.m.* bag; ~ **à dos** *n.m.* backpack; ~ **à main**
    n.m. handbag, purse; ~ **de couchage** *n.m.*
    sleeping bag

sacoche *n.f. qué.* purse, handbag
sacré *adj.* sacred
sacrer *v. qué.* swear (to) (obscenity)
sacrifier *v.* sacrifice (to)
saisir *v.* seize (to)
sale *adj.* dirty
salé *adj.* salted; salty
saler *v.* salt (to)
salir *v.* dirty (to)
salle *n.f.* room; ~ **de bain** *n.f.* bathroom
salopettes *n.f.pl.* overalls *pl.*
saluer *v.* salute (to); greet (to)
sandale *n.f.* sandal; **~s de plage** *n.f.pl.* flip flops
sandwich *n.m.* sandwich
sanitaire *adj.* sanitary
sans *prep.* without
sans-dessein *adj. qué.* idiot
saoul *adj.* drunk
satisfaire *v.* satisfy (to)
saucisse *n.f.* sausage
sauf *adj.* safe; *prep.* except
sauté *adj. qué.* crazy
sauter *v.* jump (to)
sauver *v.* save (to)
savoir *v.* know (to)
savon *n.m.* soap
sceptique *adj.* skeptical
science *n.f.* science
scier *v.* saw (to)
seau *n.m.* bucket
sec *adj.* dry
sécher *v.* dry (to)
second *adj.* second
seconde *n.f.* second
secouer *v.* shake (to)
secourir *v.* rescue (to)
sel *n.m.* salt
semaine *n.f.* week
sembler *v.* seem (to)

sentir *v.* smell (to)
séparé *adj.* separated
séparer *v.* separate (to)
serrer *v.* tighten (to); squeeze (to); shake (to)
    (hand); *qué.* put away (to)
servir *v.* serve (to)
shampoing *n.m.* shampoo
shorts *n.m.pl.* shorts *pl.*
show *n.m. inf.* show
siège *n.m.* seat
siffler *v.* whistle (to)
siffleux *n.m. qué.* woodchuck
signaler *v.* dial (to); signal (to)
signer *v.* sign (to)
signifier *v.* mean (to)
silencieux *adj.* silent, quiet
sirop *n.m.* syrup; ~ **d'érable** *n.m.* maple syrup;
    ~ **pour la toux** *n.m.* cough syrup
ski *n.m.* ski; ~ **alpin** *n.m.* downhill skiing, alpine
    skiing; ~ **de fond** *n.m.* cross-country skiing
skier *v.* ski (to)
sloche *n.f. qué.* slush
snob *adj.* snobby
snowboard *n.m.* snowboard
snowboarding *n.m.* snowboarding
soccer *n.m.* soccer
soeur *n.f.* sister
sofa *n.m. qué.* sofa, couch
soir *n.m.* evening; ce ~ *adv.* tonight
soirée *n.f.* evening
solde *n.m.* sale; balance (account)
soleil *n.m.* sun
solide *adj.* solid
sonner *v.* ring (to)
sophistiqué *adj.* sophisticated
sortie *n.f.* exit; outing
sortir *v.* go out (to); exit (to)
sou *n.m.* cent
souffler *v.* blow (to)

souffleuse *n.f. qué.* snowblower
souffrir *v.* suffer (to)
souhaiter *v.* hope (to); wish (to)
soulagé *adj.* relieved
soulier *n.m.* shoe
soumettre *v.* submit (to)
souper *n.m.* supper, dinner
soupir *n.m.* sigh
soupirer *v.* sigh (to)
sourd *adj.* deaf
sourire *n.m.* smile; *v.* smile (to)
souris *n.f.* mouse
sous *prep.* under
sous-sol *n.m.* basement
sous-vêtement *n.m.* underwear
soustraire *v.* subtract (to)
soutenir *v.* support (to)
soutien-gorge *n.m.* bra
souvenir *n.m.* souvenir; ~ **(se)** *v.* remember (to)
souvent *adv.* often
spectacle *n.m.* show
squash *n.m.* squash (sport)
stationnement *n.m.* parking
stationner *v.* park (to); ~ **(se)** *v.* park (to)
steak *n.m.* steak; ~ **haché** *n.m. qué.* ground beef
stupide *adj.* stupid
stylo *n.m.* pen
stylo-bille *n.m.* pen
sucre *n.m.* sugar
sucré *adj.* sweet; sweetened
sud *n.m.* south
sud-africain *n.m.* South African;
    adj. South African
sud-américain *n.m.* South American;
    adj. South American
suffisant *adj.* sufficient
suggérer *v.* suggest (to)
suisse *n.m.* Swiss; *adj.* Swiss
suivre *v.* follow (to)

support *n.m. qué.* coat hanger
sur *prep.* on; *adj.* sour
sûr *adj.* safe; ~ **de soi** self-confident
surprendre *v.* surprise (to)
surpris *adj.* surprised
surveiller *v.* supervise (to); watch over (to)
survivre *v.* survive (to)
suspect *adj.* suspicious
switch *n.f. qué.* switch

T

table *n.f.* table
tache *n.f.* stain
tacher *v.* stain (to)
tante *n.f.* aunt
tard *adj.* late; *adv.* late
tarte *n.f.* pie; ~ **à la farlouche** *n.f. qué.* raisin pie
tasse *n.f.* cup
taxi *n.m.* taxi
T-bar *n.m. qué.* T-bar, chairlift
technique *adj.* technical
technologique *adj.* technological
télécopieur *n.m.* fax
téléphone *n.m.* telephone
téléphoner *v.* phone (to)
télévision *n.f.* television; **chaîne de** ~ *n.f. qué.*
    tv channel
tempête *n.f.* storm; ~ **de neige** *n.f.* snowstorm
temps *n.m.* time
tendre *adj.* tender; *v.* hold out (to)
tenir *v.* hold (to)
tennis *n.m.* tennis
tente *n.f.* tent
tenter *v.* try (to); tempt (to)
terminer *v.* end (to), finish (to)
terne *adj.* drab
terrasse *n.f.* patio; terrace

tête *n.f.* head
têtu *adj.* stubborn
thé *n.m.* tea; **poche de ~** *n.f. qué.* teabag; **sachet de ~** *n.m.* teabag
théâtre *n.m.* theater
thym *n.m.* thyme
tiède *adj.* lukewarm
timbre *n.m.* stamp
tire-bouchon *n.m.* corkscrew
tirer *v.* pull (to)
toilette *n.f.* toilet
toit *n.m.* roof
tomate *n.f.* tomato
tomber *v.* fall (to)
torchon *n.m.* rag
tôt *adv.* early
total *adj.* total
toucher *v.* touch (to)
toujours *adv.* always; **pour ~** *adv.* forever
toune *n.f. qué. slang* song, tune
tourner *v.* turn (to)
tourtière *n.f. qué.* meat pie
tousser *v.* cough (to)
toux *n.f.* cough
traduction *n.f.* translation
traduire *v.* translate (to)
trahir *v.* betray (to)
train *n.m.* train
traitre *n.m.* traitor
trancher *v.* slice (to)
transformer *v.* transform (to)
transpirer *v.* perspire (to)
transporter *v.* transport (to); carry (to)
travail *n.m.* work
travaillant *adj.* hardworking
travailler *v.* work (to)
traverser *v.* cross (to) (street, river, etc.)
traversier *n.m. qué.* ferry
trembler *v.* tremble (to), shake (to)

tremper *v.* soak (to)
triathlon *n.m.* triathlon
tricher *v.* cheat (to)
tricheur *n.m.* cheat, cheater
trier *v.* sort (to)
triste *adj.* sad
troisième *adj.* third
tromper *v.* deceive (to); fool around (to)
    (spouse); ~ **(se)** make a mistake (to)
trouble *n.m.* trouble
trouver *v.* find (to)
tuer *v.* kill (to)
tuque *n.f.* tuque
turquoise *adj.* turquoise
twitte *adj. qué.* stupid

U

unique *adj.* unique
unir *v.* unite (to)
université *n.f.* university
urbain *adj.* urban
urgence *n.f.* emergency
urgent *adj.* urgent
usé *adj.* used
ustensile *n.m. qué.* utensil
utiliser *v.* use (to)

V

vache *n.f.* cow
valide *adj.* valid
valise *n.f.* suitcase; *n.f. qué.* trunk (car)
vanne *n.f. qué.* van
vantard *adj.* boastful
vanter (se) *v.* brag (to)

varier *v.* vary (to)

végétarien *n.m.* vegetarian; *adj.* vegetarian

veillée *n.f.* evening

veiller *v.* stay up late (to)

vendre *v.* sell (to)

vendu *n.m. qué.* traitor; *adj.* sold

venir *v.* come (to)

vent *n.m.* wind

vente *n.f.* sale

ventilateur *n.m.* fan

verglas *n.m.* freezing rain

vérifier *v.* verify (to)

verre *n.m.* glass

verrouillé *adj.* locked

verrouiller *v.* lock (to)

vers *prep.* toward

verser *v.* pour (to)

vert *adj.* green

vêtements *n.m.pl.* clothes *pl.*

vidanges *n.f.pl. qué.* garbage

vide *adj.* empty

vider *v.* empty (to)

vieillir *v.* grow old (to)

vietnamien *n.m.* Vietnamese; *adj.* Vietnamese

vieux *adj.* old

vin *n.m.* wine

vinaigre *n.m.* vinegar

virer *v. qué.* turn (to)

visa *n.m.* visa

visage *n.m.* face

viser *v.* aim (to)

visite *n.f.* visit

visiter *v.* visit (to)

visuel *adj.* visual

vite *adj.* fast

vitesse *n.f.* speed

vivant *adj.* alive

vivre *v.* live (to)

voile *n.f.* sailing; sail; *n.m.* veil

voir *v.* see (to)
voiture *n.f.* car
vol *n.m.* flight; theft
voler *v.* fly (to); steal (to)
volleyball *n.m.* volleyball
vomir *v.* vomit (to)
voter *v.* vote (to)
vouloir *v.* want (to)
voyager *v.* travel (to)
vrai *adj.* true

W

week-end *n.m.* weekend

Z

zipper *n.m. qué. inf.* zipper; *v. qué. inf.* zip (to)
zucchini *n.m. qué.* zucchini

ENGLISH-QUÉBÉCOIS DICTIONARY

A

abandon (to) *v.* abandonner
able *adj.* capable; be ~ (to) *v.* pouvoir
abnormal *adj.* anormal
Aboriginal *n.* autochtone *m.*; *adj.* autochtone
about *prep.* de
absolute *adj.* absolu
absurd *adj.* absurde
abuse (to) *v.* abuser
accelerate (to) *v.* accélérer
accentuate (to) *v.* accentuer
accept (to) *v.* accepter
acceptable *adj.* acceptable
accepted *adj.* admis
accompany (to) *v.* accompagner
accomplish (to) *v.* accomplir, effectuer
accomplished *adj.* accompli
accuse (to) *v.* accuser
acoustic *adj.* acoustique
acquire (to) *v.* acquérir
acquired *adj.* acquis
acrid *adj.* âcre
across *prep.* à travers; ~ from *prep.* en face de
act (to) *v.* agir
activate (to) *v.* activer
active *adj.* actif
acute *adj.* aigu
add (to) *v.* ajouter; additionner (numbers)
addition *n.* addition *f.*
address (to) *v.* adresser
adequate *adj.* adéquat
adjacent *adj.* adjacent
administer (to) *v.* administrer
admirable *adj.* admirable
admire (to) *v.* admirer
admit (to) *v.* admettre, avouer

admitted *adj.* admis
adopt (to) *v.* adopter
adore (to) *v.* adorer
adult *n.* adulte *m.*
advance (to) *v.* avancer
advanced *adj.* avancé
advise (to) *v.* conseiller
African *n.* africain *m.; adj.* africain
after *adv.* après; *prep.* après
afternoon *n.* après-midi *m.*
against *prep.* contre
agitated *adj.* énervé
aggravating *adj.* agaçant
agile *adj.* agile
agricultural *adj.* agricole
aim (to) *v.* viser
air *n.* air *m.; ~* conditioning *n.* air climatisé *m.,*
    air conditionné *m. qué.*
airplane *n.* avion *m.*
airport *n.* aéroport *m.*
ajar *adj.* entrouvert
alarm clock *n.* réveil-matin *m.,* cadran *m. qué.*
alcohol *n.* alcool *m.*
alcoholic *adj.* alcoolique; alcoolisé (beverage)
alert *adj.* alerte
alive *adj.* vivant
allow (to) *v.* permettre
always *adv.* toujours
ambiguous *adj.* ambigu
ambitious *adj.* ambitieux
ambulance *n.* ambulance *f.*
American *n.* américain *m.; adj.* américain
among *prep.* parmi
amuse (to) *v.* amuser
amusing *adj.* amusant
analgesic *adj.* analgésique
ancient *adj.* ancien
and *conj.* et
announce (to) *v.* annoncer

annoy (to) *v.* ennuyer
annoying *adj.* achalant *qué.*, agaçant
annual *adj.* annuel
answer *n.* réponse *f.*; ~ **(to)** *v.* répondre
antiseptic *adj.* antiseptique
anxious *adj.* anxieux
appear (to) *v.* apparaître; paraître
applaud (to) *v.* applaudir
apple *n.* pomme *f.*
apply (to) *v.* appliquer
appointment *n.* rendez-vous *m.*
appreciate (to) *v.* apprécier
approach (to) *v.* approcher
approve (to) *v.* approuver
approximately *adv.* environ
apricot *n.* abricot *m.*
Arab *n.* arabe *m.*; *adj.* arabe
Arabian *n.* arabe *m.*; *adj.* arabe
Arabic *n.* arabe *m.*; *adj.* arabe
archaic *adj.* archaïque
architecture *n.* architecture *f.*
arduous *adj.* ardu
arena *n.* aréna *m.*
argue (to) *v.* chicaner (se), astiner (s') *qué. slang*
argument *n.* chicane *f. qué.*
arid *adj.* aride
arm *n.* bras *m.*
around *prep.* autour de
arrange (to) *v.* arranger
arrest (to) *v.* arrêter
arrive (to) *v.* arriver
arrogant *adj.* arrogant
art *n.* art *m.*
artistic *adj.* artistique
ascend (to) *v.* monter
Asian *n.* asiatique *m.*; *adj.* oriental, asiatique
ask (to) *v.* demander
assemble (to) *v.* assembler
associate with (to) *v.* fréquenter; associer (s')

assure (to) *v.* assurer
astounding *adj.* abracadabrant
astronomy *n.* astronomie *f.*
astute *adj.* astucieux
at *prep.* à; chez (somebody's)
athletic *adj.* athlétique
ATM *n.* guichet automatique *m.*
attach (to) *v.* attacher
attack (to) *v.* attaquer
attract (to) *v.* attirer
aunt *n.* tante *f.*; matante *f. qué. inf.*
Australian *n.* australien *m.*; *adj.* australien
authorize (to) *v.* autoriser
automatic *adj.* automatique
autumn *n.* automne *m.*
average *n.* moyenne *f.*; *adj.* moyen
avoid (to) *v.* éviter

B

baby *n.* bébé *m.*
babysit (to) *v.* garder
back *n.* dos *m.*; ~ **up (to)** *v.* reculer
backpack *n.* sac à dos *m.*
bacon *n.* bacon *m.*
bad *adj.* mauvais
bag *n.* sac *m.*
balance *n.* équilibre *m.*; solde *m.* (account)
balcony *n.* galerie *f. qué.*, balcon *m.*
ball *n.* ballon *m.*; balle *f.*
banana *n.* banane *f.*
bank *n.* banque *f.*; ~ **machine** *n.* guichet
    automatique *m.*
baseball *n.* baseball *m.*; ~ **cap** *n.* calotte *f. qué.*
    inf., casquette *f.*
basement *n.* cave *f. qué.*, sous-sol *m.*
basil *n.* basilic *m.*
basketball *n.* basketball *m.*

bath *n.* bain *m.*

bathing suit *n.* costume de bain *m.* *qué.*, maillot de bain *m.*

bathroom *n.* salle de bain *f.*, chambre de bain *f.* *qué.*, bécosses *f.pl. qué. slang*

battle *n.* bataille *f.*

be (to) *v.* être

beach *n.* plage *f.*

bean *n.* fève *f.*; haricot *m.*; **baked ~s** *n.* fèves au lard *f.pl. qué.*; binnes *f.pl. qué.*

bear *n.* ours *m.*

bearded *adj.* barbu

beat (to) *v.* planter (someone) *qué. slang*, battre

beautiful *adj.* beau

beaver *n.* castor *m.*

because *conj.* car

become (to) *v.* devenir

bed *n.* lit *m.*; **put to ~ (to)** *v.* coucher; **go to ~ (to)** *v.* coucher (se)

bedroom *n.* chambre à coucher *f.*

beef *n.* boeuf *m.*; **ground ~** *n.* boeuf haché *m.*, steak haché *m. qué.*

beer *n.* bière *f.*; **draft ~** *n.* bière pression *f.*, bière en fût *f. qué.*, draff *f. qué. inf.*

beet *n.* betterave *f.*

before *adv.* avant; *prep.* avant

beg (to) *v.* mendier (for money)

begin (to) *v.* commencer

behind *prep.* derrière

believe (to) *v.* croire, craire *qué. inf.*

belong (to) *v.* appartenir

beluga *n.* béluga *m.*

bend (to) *v.* plier; **~ over (to)** *v.* pencher (se)

beside *prep.* à côté de

best *n.* meilleur *m.*

bet *n.* pari *m.*; **~ (to)** *v.* gager *qué.*, parier

betray (to) *v.* trahir

better *adj.* meilleur

between *prep.* entre

biathlon *n.* biathlon *m.*

bicycle *n.* bicyclette *f.*, bicycle *m. qué.*

big *adj.* gros

bill *n.* facture *f.*; addition *f.*

bird *n.* oiseau *m.*

bite (to) *v.* mordre

bitter *adj.* amer

bittersweet *adj.* aigre-doux

black *adj.* noir

blame (to) *v.* blâmer

blanket *n.* couverte *f. qué.*, couverture *f.*

blend (to) *v.* mélanger

blind *adj.* aveugle

blow (to) *v.* souffler

blue *adj.* bleu

blueberry *n.* bleuet *m.*

blush (to) *v.* rougir

boastful *adj.* vantard

boat *n.* bateau *m.*

boil (to) *v.* bouillir

boiled *adj.* bouilli

boiling *adj.* bouillant

book *n.* livre *m.*

boot *n.* botte *f.*

bore (to) *v.* ennuyer

boring *adj.* plate *qué.*, ennuyant, ennuyeux

born (to be) *v.* naître

borrow (to) *v.* emprunter

bother (to) *v.* achaler *qué.*, gêner

bothersome *adj.* achalant *qué.*, gênant

bought *adj.* acheté

bowl *n.* bol *m.*

box *n.* boîte *f.*

boy *n.* garçon *m.*

boyfriend *n.* chum *m. qué. inf.*, petit ami *m.*, copain *m.*

bra *n.* brassière *f. qué.*, soutien-gorge *m.*

brag (to) *v.* vanter (se)

bread *n.* pain *m.*

break (to) *v.* casser, briser, péter *qué. inf.;* ~ **up**
  (to) *v.* casser *qué.,* rompre (relationship)
breakfast *n.* déjeuner *m. qué.,* petit déjeuner *m.*
breathe (to) *v.* respirer
bring (to) *v.* amener, apporter; ~ **back (to)**
  v. ramener, rapporter; ~ **closer (to)**
  v. rapprocher
broad *adj.* ample
broccoli *n.* brocoli *m.*
broken *adj.* brisé, cassé, pété *qué. inf.*
brother *n.* frère *m.*
brother-in-law *n.* beau-frère *m.*
brown *adj.* brun, marron
brush *n.* brosse *f.;* ~ **(to)** *v.* brosser
buck *n.* piasse *f. qué. inf.,* piastre *f. qué. inf.*
  (money)
bucket *n.* seau *m.*
bug *n.* bibitte *f. qué. inf.,* insecte *m.,* moustique *m.;*
  ~ **repellent** *n.* chasse-moustiques *m.*
build (to) *v.* construire
bullfrog *n.* ouaouaron *m. qué.*
burn (to) *v.* brûler
bury (to) *v.* enterrer
bus *n.* autobus *m.*
busy *adj.* achalandé (establishment); engagé *qué.*
  (telephone line); occupé
but *conj.* mais
butter *n.* beurre *m.;* **peanut** ~ *n.* beurre de
  pinottes *m. qué.,* beurre d'arachides *m.*
buy (to) *v.* acheter
by *prep.* par

C

cabbage *n.* chou *m.*
cake *n.* gâteau *m.*
calculate (to) *v.* calculer
calculator *n.* calculatrice *f.*

calendar *n.* calendrier *m.*

call *n.* appel *m.*; ~ **(to)** *v.* appeler

calm *adj.* calme; ~ **(to)** *v.* calmer

calorie *n.* calorie *f.*

camp *n.* camp *m.*; **summer** ~ *n.* camp de
    vacances *m. qué.*, colonie de vacances *f.*;
    ~ **(to)** *v.* camper

can *n.* canette *f. qué.*; boîte de conserve *f.*, can *f.*
    qué.; ~ **opener** *n.* ouvre-boîte *m.*

Canadian *n.* canadien *m.*; *adj.* canadien

candle *n.* bougie *f.*, chandelle *f.*

cane *n.* canne *f.*

canoe *n.* canot *m. qué.*, canoë *m.*

cantaloupe *n.* cantaloup *m.*

canteen *n.* gourde *f.*

capable *adj.* capable

car *n.* auto *f.*, char *m. inf.*, voiture *f.*, automobile *f.*

carbonated *adj.* gazeux

card *n.* carte *f.*; **credit** ~ *n.* carte de crédit *f.*

carnivore *n.* carnivore *m.*

carnivorous *adj.* carnivore

carrot *n.* carotte *f.*

carry (to) *v.* porter, transporter; ~ **out (to)**
    v. effectuer

cash *n.* argent comptant *m.*, bidou *m. qué. inf.*

casino *n.* casino *m.*

cat *n.* chat *m.*

catch (to) *v.* attraper

cauliflower *n.* chou-fleur *m.*

cause (to) *v.* causer

cave *n.* caverne *f.*

ceiling *n.* plafond *m.*

celebrate (to) *v.* célébrer

celery *n.* céleri *m.*

cent *n.* cenne *f. qué.*, sou *m.*

center *n.* centre *m.*

cereal *n.* céréales *f.pl.*

chair *n.* chaise *f.*

chairlift *n.* T-bar *m. qué.*, remonte-pente *m.*

change *n.* change *m. qué.*, monnaie *f.* (money);
~ **(to)** *v.* changer

channel *n.* canal *m.*, chaîne de télévision *f.*
qué. (tv)

charge (to) *v.* charger

chase (to) *v.* chasser

chat (to) *v.* jaser *qué.*, bavarder, causer,
placoter *qué.*

cheat *n.* tricheur *m.*; ~ **(to)** *v.* tricher

cheater *n.* tricheur *m.*

check *n.* chèque *m.*; **traveler's** ~ *n.* chèque de
voyage *m.*

cheerful *adj.* joyeux

cheese *n.* fromage *m.*

cheesy *adj.* quétaine *qué.*

chemistry *n.* chimie *f.*

cherry *n.* cerise *f.*

chestnut *n.* marron *m.*

chew (to) *v.* mâcher

chicken *n.* poulet *m.*

chickpea *n.* pois chiche *m.*

child *n.* enfant *m.*, flo *m. qué. inf.*

chill (to) *v.* refroidir

Chinese *n.* chinois *m.*; *adj.* chinois

chives *n.* ciboulette *f.*

chocolate *n.* chocolat *m.*; ~ **bar** *n.* palette de
chocolat *f. qué.*, tablette de chocolat *f.*

choose (to) *v.* choisir

Christmas log *n.* bûche de Noël *f. qué.*

circus *n.* cirque *m.*

citizen *n.* citoyen *m.*

citizenship *n.* citoyenneté *f.*

clean *adj.* propre; ~ **(to)** *v.* nettoyer

climb (to) *v.* grimper; monter

close *adv.* près; ~ **(to)** *v.* fermer; ~ **to** *prep.* près de

closed *adj.* fermé

clothes *n.pl.* vêtements *m.pl.*

cloud *n.* nuage *m.*

cloudy *adj.* nuageux

coat *n.* manteau *m.*; ~ **hanger** *n.* support *m. qué.*,
    cintre *m.*
coffee *n.* café *m.*
coin *n.* pièce *f.*
coincidence *n.* adon *m. qué.*, coïncidence *f.*
cold *n.* froid *m.* (temperature); rhume *m.*
    (illness); *adj.* froid, frette *qué. slang*
comb *n.* peigne *m.*; ~ **(to)** *v.* peigner
combine **(to)** *v.* combiner
come **(to)** *v.* venir; ~ **back (to)** *v.* revenir
comforter *n.* couette *f.*
command **(to)** *v.* commander
communicate **(to)** *v.* communiquer
compare **(to)** *v.* comparer
complain **(to)** *v.* critiquer, plaindre (se), bitcher
    qué. slang, chialer *qué.*
complete *adj.* complet; ~ **(to)** *v.* compléter
compose **(to)** *v.* composer
computer *n.* ordinateur *m.*
conceive **(to)** *v.* concevoir
concerned *adj.* inquiet
conclude **(to)** *v.* conclure
conduct **(to)** *v.* diriger (orchestra)
confess **(to)** *v.* confesser, avouer
confide **(to)** *v.* confier (se)
confirm **(to)** *v.* confirmer
confused *adj.* mêlé *qué.*, confus
congratulate **(to)** *v.* féliciter
consider **(to)** *v.* considérer
console **(to)** *v.* consoler
consulate *n.* consulat *m.*
consult **(to)** *v.* consulter
contain **(to)** *v.* contenir
continue **(to)** *v.* continuer
contribute **(to)** *v.* contribuer
convenience store *n.* dépanneur *m. qué.*
convince **(to)** *v.* convaincre
cook **(to)** *v.* cuire; cuisiner
cooked *adj.* cuit
cool *adj.* frais; ~ **(to)** *v.* refroidir

cooperate (to) *v.* coopérer

copy (to) *v.* copier

corkscrew *n.* tire-bouchon *m.*

corn *n.* blé d'Inde *m. qué.*, maïs *m.*; ~ **roast** *n.*
    épluchette *f. qué.*, épluchette de blé d'Inde
    f. qué.

cost (to) *v.* coûter

cottage *n.* chalet *m.*

couch *n.* sofa *m. qué.*, divan *m.*, canapé *m.*

cough *n.* toux *f.*; ~ **(to)** *v.* tousser

count (to) *v.* compter

cousin *n.* cousin *m.*

cover (to) *v.* couvrir; ~ **oneself (to)** *v.* abriller (s')
    qué.

covered *adj.* couvert

cow *n.* vache *f.*

cranberry *n.* atoca *m. qué.*, canneberge *f.*

crawl (to) *v.* ramper

crazy *adj.* fou, sauté *qué.*, malade *qué.*

cream *n.* crème *f.*; **hand** ~ *n.* crème à mains *f.*;
    ice ~ *n.* crème glacée *f.*

creamy *adj.* crémeux

create (to) *v.* créer

creative *adj.* créatif

crepe *n.* crêpe *f.*

cross (to) *v.* traverser (street, river, etc.); ~ **out**
    (to) *v.* barrer

crush (to) *v.* écraser; écrapoutir *qué. slang*

cry (to) *v.* pleurer, brailler *qué. inf.*

crybaby *n.* bébé la-la *m. qué.*

cucumber *n.* concombre *m.*

cultivate (to) *v.* cultiver

cup *n.* tasse *f.*

cure (to) *v.* guérir

curling *n.* curling *m.*

custard *n.* costarde *f. qué.*

cut (to) *v.* couper

cutlery *n.* coutellerie *f.*

cycling *n.* cyclisme *m.*

D

daily *adj.* quotidien
dampen (to) *v.* mouiller
dance (to) *v.* danser
dare (to) *v.* oser
darkness *n.* noirceur *f. qué.*
date *n.* datte *f.* (fruit); date *f.* (day); rendez-vous *m.*;
    ~ **(to)** *v.* fréquenter
daughter *n.* fille *f.*
day *n.* jour *m.*, journée *f.*
dead *adj.* mort
deaf *adj.* sourd
dear *adj.* cher
debate (to) *v.* débattre
deceive (to) *v.* tromper
decide (to) *v.* décider
declare (to) *v.* déclarer
decorate (to) *v.* décorer
decrease (to) *v.* baisser, diminuer, réduire
deer *n.* chevreuil *m.*, cerf de virginie *m.*
defend (to) *v.* défendre
delete (to) *v.* effacer
deliver (to) *v.* livrer
demand (to) *v.* exiger
demolish (to) *v.* démolir
dental *adj.* dentaire
deny (to) *v.* nier
depend (to) *v.* dépendre
deposit (to) *v.* déposer
deprive (to) *v.* priver
descend (to) *v.* descendre
describe (to) *v.* décrire
deserve (to) *v.* mériter
desire (to) *v.* désirer
destroy (to) *v.* détruire
detach (to) *v.* détacher
determine (to) *v.* déterminer
detest (to) *v.* détester

develop (to) *v.* développer
devour (to) *v.* dévorer
dial (to) *v.* signaler, composer
diamond *n.* diamant *m.*
dictionary *n.* dictionnaire *m.*
die (to) *v.* mourir
difficult *adj.* difficile
dig (to) *v.* creuser
dill *n.* aneth *m.*
diminish (to) *v.* diminuer, réduire
dinner *n.* souper *m.*
direct (to) *v.* diriger
dirty *adj.* sale; ~ **(to)** *v.* salir
disabled *adj.* handicapé
disappear (to) *v.* disparaître
disappointed *adj.* déçu
disco *n.* discothèque *f.*, boîte de nuit *f.*
discourage (to) *v.* décourager
discover (to) *v.* découvrir
discuss (to) *v.* discuter
disguise (to) *v.* déguiser
disgusting *adj.* dégueulasse *inf.*, dégoûtant
disobey (to) *v.* désobéir
disregard (to) *v.* négliger
distinguish (to) *v.* distinguer
distribute (to) *v.* distribuer
dive (to) *v.* plonger
divide (to) *v.* diviser
divorced *adj.* divorcé
do (to) *v.* faire
doctor *n.* médecin *m.*
dog *n.* chien *m.*
door *n.* porte *f.*
double (to) *v.* doubler
doubt (to) *v.* douter
doughnut *n.* beigne *m. qué.*, beignet *m.*
drab *adj.* terne
draw (to) *v.* dessiner
dream (to) *v.* rêver

drench (to) *v.* tremper, mouiller
dress *n.* robe *f.*; ~ **(to)** *v.* habiller; habiller (s')
    (oneself)
dressed *adj.* habillé
drink (to) *v.* boire
drive (to) *v.* conduire
drop (to) *v.* échapper
drunk *adj.* paqueté *qué. slang*, chaud *qué.*,
    saoul, ivre
dry *adj.* sec; ~ **cleaner** *n.* nettoyeur *m. qué.*;
    ~ **(to)** *v.* essuyer; sécher
duck *n.* canard *m.*; ~ **(to)** *v.* baisser (se)
dull *adj.* dull *qué. slang*, ennuyeux, ennuyant
dumb *adj.* épais *qué.*
during *prep.* pendant, durant
dusk *n.* brunante *f. qué.*, crépuscule *m.*
Dutch *n.* hollandais *m.*; *adj.* hollandais
duvet *n.* douillette *f. qué.*, duvet *m.*, couette *f.*

E

ear *n.* oreille *f.*
early *adv.* tôt
earring *n.* boucle d'oreille *f.*
east *n.* est *m.*
eastern *adj.* oriental
easy *adj.* facile
easygoing *adj.* accommodant
eat (to) *v.* manger, bouffer *inf.*
economy *n.* économie *f.*
edible *adj.* comestible
effective *adj.* efficace
efficient *adj.* efficace
egg *n.* oeuf *m.*
eggplant *n.* aubergine *f.*
egocentric *adj.* égocentrique
egotistical *adj.* égoïste

elaborate *adj.* approfondi, élaboré
elder *n.* aîné *m.*
eldest *adj.* aîné
elect (to) *v.* élire
electric *adj.* électrique
electrical *adj.* électrique
electricity *n.* électricité *f.*
electronic *adj.* électronique
e-mail *n.* courriel *m. qué.*
embarrass (to) *v.* gêner
embarrassed *adj.* gêné
embarrassing *adj.* gênant
embassy *n.* ambassade *f.*
emergency *n.* urgence *f.*
emigrate (to) *v.* émigrer
employ (to) *v.* employer
empty *adj.* vide; ~ **(to)** *v.* vider
encourage (to) *v.* encourager
end *n.* fin *f.*; ~ **(to)** *v.* terminer, finir
engaged *adj.* fiancé
engineering *n.* génie *m.*
English *n.* anglais *m.*; *adj.* anglais
enter (to) *v.* entrer
entice (to) *v.* attirer
entrust (to) *v.* confier
envelop (to) *v.* envelopper
envelope *n.* enveloppe *f.*
envied *adj.* envié
erase (to) *v.* effacer
escort (to) *v.* accompagner
establish (to) *v.* établir
estimate (to) *v.* estimer
European *n.* européen; *adj.* européen
evening *n.* soirée *f.*, soir *m.*; veillée *f.*
exaggerate (to) *v.* exagérer
examine (to) *v.* examiner
excellent *adj.* excellent
except *prep.* sauf, excepté

exchange (to) *v.* échanger
exciting *adj.* excitant
excuse (to) *v.* excuser
exhaust (to) *v.* épuiser
exist (to) *v.* exister
exit *n.* sortie *f.*; ~ (to) *v.* sortir
expensive *adj.* cher, coûteux, dispendieux
explain (to) *v.* expliquer
export (to) *v.* exporter
extinguish (to) *v.* éteindre
eye *n.* oeil *m.* (plural: yeux)
eyeglasses *n.* lunettes *f.pl.*, barniques *f.pl. qué.*

F

face *n.* visage *m.*, face *f.*, bette *f. qué.*
facecloth *n.* débarbouillette *f. qué.*
fail (to) *v.* échouer
faint (to) *v.* évanouir (s')
fall *n.* automne *m.* (season); ~ (to) *v.* tomber
false *adj.* faux
family *n.* famille *f.*
famished *adj.* affamé
fan *n.* ventilateur *m.*
far *adj.* loin; ~ from *prep.* loin de
farm *n.* ferme *f.*
fast *adj.* rapide, vite
fat *n.* gras *m.*; *adj.* gras, gros
father *n.* père *m.*
father-in-law *n.* beau-père *m.*
faucet *n.* champlure *f. qué. inf.*, robinet *m.*
favorite *adj.* préféré
fax *n.* télécopieur *m.*
fear *n.* peur *f.*; ~ (to) *v.* craindre, avoir peur
feed (to) *v.* nourrir; nourrir (se) (oneself)
feel (to) *v.* ressentir
fencing *n.* escrime *m.*
ferry *n.* traversier *m. qué.*

fiancé *n.* fiancé *m.*
fig *n.* figue *f.*
fight *n.* bataille *f.*; ~ (to) *v.* battre (se)
fill (to) *v.* remplir
find (to) *v.* trouver; ~ again (to) *v.* retrouver
finger *n.* doigt *m.*
finish (to) *v.* finir, terminer; aboutir
fire *n.* feu *m.*; camp~ *n.* feu de camp *m.*; ~ (to)
    v. congédier (employee)
firefly *n.* mouche à feu *f. qué.*, luciole *f.*
fireplace *n.* foyer *m.*
firm *adj.* ferme
first *adj.* premier
fish *n.* poisson *m.*; ~ (to) *v.* pêcher
fishing *n.* pêche *f.*
fix (to) *v.* réparer
flashlight *n.* lampe de poche *f.*
flatten (to) *v.* aplatir, écraser, effoirer *qué.*
flawless *adj.* impeccable
flee (to) *v.* fuir, enfuir (s')
flight *n.* vol *m.*
flip-flops *n.* gougounes *f.pl. qué.*, sandales de
    plage *f.pl.*
float (to) *v.* flotter
flood *n.* inondation *f.*; ~ (to) *v.* inonder
floor *n.* plancher *m.*; étage *m.*;
    first ~ *n.* rez-de-chaussée *m.*
florist *n.* fleuriste *m.*
flower *n.* fleur *f.*
fluctuate (to) *v.* fluctuer
fly *n.* mouche *f.*; ~ (to) *v.* voler
follow (to) *v.* suivre
food *n.* nourriture *f.*, bouffe *f. inf.*, manger *m.*
fool around (to) *v.* tromper (spouse)
foot *n.* pied *m.*
football *n.* football *m.* (American)
for *prep.* pour; *conj.* car
forbid (to) *v.* défendre, interdire
force (to) *v.* forcer

forecast (to) *v*. prévoir
foresee (to) *v*. prévoir
forever *adv*. pour toujours
forge (to) *v*. forger
forget (to) *v*. oublier
forgive (to) *v*. pardonner
fork *n*. fourchette *f*.
form (to) *v*. former
former *adj*. ancien
fox *n*. renard *m*.
freeze (to) *v*. geler
French *n*. français *m*.; *adj*. français; ~ fry *n*.
    patate frite *f*. *qué.*, frite *f*.
frequent *adj*. fréquent
fresh *adj*. frais
fried *adj*. frit
friend *n*. ami *m*.
frightened *adj*. apeuré
from *prep*. de
front *n*. devant *m*.; in ~ of *prep*. devant
frozen *adj*. gelé
fruit *n*. fruit *m*.; passion ~ *n*. fruit de la passion *m*.
fruitful *adj*. fructueux
fudge *n*. fudge *m*. *qué.*, fondant au chocolat *m*.
full *adj*. plein
funny *adj*. drôle
furnace *n*. fournaise *f*.

G

gallery *n*. galerie *f*.
galoshes *n*. claques *f.pl.* *qué.*
garbage *n*. vidanges *f.pl.* *qué.*, ordure *f*., déchet *m*.
garden *n*. jardin *m*.
gas *n*. gaz *m*. *qué.*, essence *f*.
general store *n*. dépanneur *m*. *qué.*
gentle *adj*. doux
geography *n*. géographie *f*.

geology *n.* géologie *f.*
German *n.* allemand *m.*; *adj.* allemand
get (to) *v.* procurer (se); ~ **along (to)** *v.* adonner
   (s') *qué.*, accorder (s'); ~ **lost (to)** *v.* écarter
   (s') *qué.*, perdre (se); ~ **off (to)** *v.* débarquer;
   ~ **on (to)** *v.* monter (bike, horse),
   embarquer
gift *n.* cadeau *m.*
girl *n.* fille *f.*
girlfriend *n.* blonde *f. qué. inf.*, petite amie *f.*,
   copine *f.*
give (to) *v.* donner; ~ **back (to)** *v.* rendre,
   remettre, redonner
glass *n.* verre *m.*; **wine** ~ *n.* coupe *f.*; ~ **of wine** *n.*
   coupe de vin *f.*
glimpse (to) *v.* apercevoir; entrevoir
global *adj.* global
glow (to) *v.* luire
glue *n.* colle *f.*; ~ **(to)** *v.* coller
gluttonous *adj.* gourmand, glouton
go (to) *v.* aller; ~ **back (to)** *v.* retourner; ~ **down**
   (to) *v.* descendre; ~ **out (to)** *v.* sortir; ~ **up**
   (to) *v.* monter
gold *n.* or *m.*; *adj.* or
good *adj.* bon
good-natured *adj.* accommodant
goose *n.* oie *f.*; **Canada** ~ *n.* outarde *f. qué.*
grandfather *n.* grand-père *m.*
grandmother *n.* grand-mère *f.*
grape *n.* raisin *m.*
grapefruit *n.* pamplemousse *m.*
gray *adj.* gris
Greek *n.* grec *m.*; *adj.* grec
green *adj.* vert
greet (to) *v.* accueillir; saluer
grow (to) *v.* grandir; ~ **old (to)** *v.* vieillir;
   ~ **up (to)** *v.* grandir
growl (to) *v.* grogner
grunt (to) *v.* grogner

guarantee (to) *v.* garantir
guess (to) *v.* deviner
guide *n.* guide *m.*; ~ **(to)** *v.* guider
guinea pig *n.* cochon d'Inde *m.*
gymnastics *n.pl.* gymnastique *f.*

H

hair *n.* cheveux *m.pl.*
hairbrush *n.* brosse à cheveux *f.*
haircut *n.* coupe de cheveux *f.*
ham *n.* jambon *m.*
hand *n.* main *f.*
handbag *n.* sacoche *f. qué.*, sac à main *m.*,
      bourse *f.*
hangover *n.* gueule de bois *f.*
happy *adj.* heureux
hardworking *adj.* travaillant
hat *n.* chapeau *m.*
hate (to) *v.* haïr, détester
hated *adj.* haï
have (to) *v.* avoir
head *n.* tête *f.*
heal (to) *v.* guérir
hear (to) *v.* entendre
heat *n.* chaleur *f.*; ~ **(to)** *v.* chauffer
heavy *adj.* pesant, lourd
help (to) *v.* aider
here *adv.* ici, icitte *qué. slang*
hesitate (to) *v.* hésiter
hide (to) *v.* cacher
hideous *adj.* affreux
high *adj.* haut (height)
highway *n.* autoroute *f.*
hire (to) *v.* embaucher, engager
history *n.* histoire *f.*
hit (to) *v.* frapper

hitchhike (to) *v.* faire du pouce *qué.*, faire de
 l'auto-stop
hockey *n.* hockey *m.*; ~ **puck** *n.* poque *f. qué.*
 slang, rondelle *f.*
hold (to) *v.* tenir; ~ **out (to)** *v.* tendre
hope (to) *v.* espérer, souhaiter
horrible *adj.* horrible
horse *n.* cheval *m.*
hospital *n.* hôpital *m.*
hot *adj.* chaud
hot dog *n.* chien chaud *m. qué.*, hot-dog *m.*
hotel *n.* hôtel *m.*
hour *n.* heure *f.*
house *n.* maison *f.*
humiliate (to) *v.* humilier
hungry *adj.* affamé
hunt (to) *v.* chasser
hurry up (to) *v.* dépêcher (se), déguédiner (se) *qué.*
hurt *adj.* blessé; ~ **(to)** *v.* blesser
hygienic *adj.* hygiénique

I

icing *n.* crèmage *m. qué.*, glaçage *m.*
idea *n.* idée *f.*, flash *m. qué.*
idiot *n.* sans-dessein *m. qué.*, nono *qué. slang,*
 niaiseux, niais, idiot
ignorant *adj.* ignorant
ignore (to) *v.* ignorer
illuminate (to) *v.* illuminer
illustrated *adj.* illustré
imagine (to) *v.* imaginer
imbecile *adj.* imbécile
imitate (to) *v.* imiter
immediate *adj.* immédiat
immigrate (to) *v.* immigrer
impeccable *adj.* impeccable
imperative *adj.* impératif

import (to) *v.* importer
impose (to) *v.* imposer
improved *adj.* amélioré
improvise (to) *v.* improviser
in *prep.* dans; en; à
incline (to) *v.* pencher
include (to) *v.* inclure
increase (to) *v.* augmenter, hausser
indicate (to) *v.* indiquer
inedible *adj.* immangeable
inevitable *adj.* inévitable
inflate (to) *v.* gonfler
inform (to) *v.* informer, renseigner
inherit (to) *v.* hériter
injured *adj.* blessé
insect *n.* bibitte *f. qué.*, insecte *m.*, moustique *m.*
inspire (to) *v.* inspirer
install (to) *v.* installer
instruct (to) *v.* instruire
insulted *adj.* insulté
insulting *adj.* insultant
insure (to) *v.* assurer
intelligent *adj.* intelligent
interesting *adj.* intéressant
intermission *n.* intermission *f. qué.*, entracte *f.*
interrogate (to) *v.* interroger
interrupt (to) *v.* interrompre
intersection *n.* intersection *f.*
introduce (to) *v.* introduire; présenter
invade (to) *v.* envahir
invent (to) *v.* inventer
investigate (to) *v.* examiner, enquêter
invite (to) *v.* inviter
inviting *adj.* invitant
iron *n.* fer *m.* (metal); fer à repasser *m.*
        (appliance); ~ (to) *v.* repasser
irritate (to) *v.* agacer, irriter
isolate (to) *v.* isoler
Italian *n.* italien *m.*; *adj.* italien

J

jalopy *n*. minoune *f. qué. inf.*, bazou *m. qué. inf.*,
   bagnole *f. inf.*
Japanese *n*. japonais *m*.; *adj*. japonais
jazz club *n*. boîte de jazz *f*.
job *n*. job *f. qué.*
join (to) *v*. joindre
joke *n*. joke *f. qué.*, blague *f*.
juice *n*. jus *m*.
juicy *adj*. juteux
jump (to) *v*. sauter

K

kayak *n*. kayak *m*.
keep (to) *v*. garder
kettle *n*. canard *m. qué.*, bouilloire *f*.
key *n*. clé *f*.
kill (to) *v*. tuer
kind *adj*. fin *qué.*, aimable
kiss *n*. bec *m. qué.*, baiser *m*.; ~ **(to)** *v*. embrasser
kitsch *adj*. quétaine *qué.*, kitsch
kiwi *n*. kiwi *m*.
kneel (to) *v*. agenouiller (s')
knife *n*. couteau *m*.
know (to) *v*. connaître; savoir

L

lack (to) *v*. manquer
lamp *n*. lampe *f*.
language *n*. langue *f*.
last *adj*. dernier; ~ **(to)** *v*. durer
late *adj*. tard; *adv*. tard
laugh (to) *v*. rire

laundromat *n.* buanderie *f. qué.*
law *n.* droit *m.*; loi *f.*
lay down (to) *v.* coucher, étendre
lazy *adj.* flanc-mou *qué.*, paresseux
lead (to) *v.* conduire, diriger
lean *adj.* maigre
learn (to) *v.* apprendre
lease *n.* bail *m.* (apartment); ~ **(to)** *v.* louer
leased *adj.* loué
least *adj.* moindre
leave (to) *v.* laisser; partir; quitter
left *n.* gauche *f.* (direction)
leg *n.* jambe *f.*
lemon *n.* citron *m.*
lend (to) *v.* prêter
let go (to) *v.* lâcher
letter *n.* lettre *f.*
lettuce *n.* laitue *f.*
lick (to) *v.* lècher, licher *qué.*
lie (to) *v.* mentir; ~ **down (to)** *v.* coucher (se),
         allonger (s')
lift (to) *v.* lever
light *n.* lumière *f.*; **traffic** ~ *n.* lumière *f. qué.*,
         feu de circulation *m.*; *adj.* léger; pale; ~ **(to)**
         v. allumer
like (to) *v.* aimer
lilac *n.* lilas *m.*; *adj.* lilas
lime *n.* lime *f.*
limited *adj.* limité
liqueur *n.* liqueur *f.*
liquid *n.* liquide *m.*; *adj.* liquide
listen (to) *v.* écouter
literature *n.* littérature *f.*
little *adj.* petit
live (to) *v.* vivre; ~ **in (to)** *v.* habiter
lock (to) *v.* barrer *qué.*, verrouiller
locked *adj.* barré *qué.*, verrouillé
long *adj.* long; ~ **johns** *n.* combines *f.pl. qué.*

look (to) *v.* regarder; ~ for (to) *v.* chercher
loon *n.* huard *m.*
lose (to) *v.* perdre
lost *adj.* perdu; get ~ (to) *v.* perdre (se)
love *n.* amour *m.;* ~ (to) *v.* aimer
loved *adj.* aimé
loving *adj.* amoureux
low *adj.* bas
lower (to) *v.* baisser
lukewarm *adj.* tiède
lullaby *n.* berceuse *f.*
lunch *n.* dîner *m. qué.*, lunch *m.*
lure (to) *v.* attirer
luxurious *adj.* luxueux

M

mail *n.* malle *f. qué.*, courrier *m.*
maintain (to) *v.* maintenir
make (to) *v.* faire
mango *n.* mangue *f.*
manual *n.* manuel *m.; adj.* manuel
manufacture (to) *v.* fabriquer
mark (to) *v.* marquer
marketing *n.* marketing *m.*
married *adj.* marié
marry (to) *v.* marier, épouser
master (to) *v.* maîtriser
match *n.* allumette *f.*
mathematics *n.pl.* mathématiques *f. pl.*
meal *n.* repas *m.*
mean *adj.* méchant; ~ (to) *v.* signifier
measure *n.* mesure *f.;* ~ (to) *v.* mesurer
medecine *n.* médecine *f.*
medical *adj.* médical
medium *adj.* moyen
meet (to) *v.* rencontrer

melancholy *adj.* mélancolique
melody *n.* mélodie *f.*
melt (to) *v.* fondre
merry *adj.* joyeux
microwave *n.* micro-ondes *m.*
mileage *n.* millage *m.*, kilométrage *m.*
milk *n.* lait *m.*
minute *n.* minute *f.*
mirror *n.* miroir *m.*
miss (to) *v.* manquer
mistake *n.* erreur *f.*; **make a ~ (to)** *v.* tromper (se)
mitt *n.* mitaine *f.*
mitten *n.* mitaine *f.*
mix (to) *v.* mélanger
modern *adj.* moderne
moisten (to) *v.* mouiller
money *n.* argent *m.*, bidou *m. qué. inf.*
monthly *adj.* mensuel
moon *n.* lune *f.*
moose *n.* orignal *m.*
morning *n.* matin *m.*, avant-midi *m.*
mosquito *n.* maringouin *m.*
mother *n.* mère *f.*
mother-in-law *n.* belle-mère *f.*
motorcycle *n.* bicycle à gaz *m. qué.*,
      motocyclette *f.*
mouse *n.* souris *f.*
mouth *n.* bouche *f.*
move (to) *v.* bouger; déménager (residence)
movie *n.* film *m.*
mud *n.* bouette *f. qué. inf.*, boue *f.*
multiple *adj.* multiple
multiply (to) *v.* multiplier
museum *n.* musée *m.*
mushroom *n.* champignon *m.*
music *n.* musique *f.*
musical *adj.* musical
mute *adj.* muet

N

nail *n.* ongle *m.* (finger/toe); clou *m.* (hammer);
    ~ **(to)** *v.* clouer
naked *adj.* nu
name *n.* nom *m.*; ~ **(to)** *v.* nommer
nationality *n.* nationalité *f.*
Native *n.* autochtone *m.*; *adj.* autochtone
near *adj.* près
neck *n.* cou *m.*
necklace *n.* collier *m.*
nectarine *n.* nectarine *f.*
neglect (to) *v.* négliger
neighboring *adj.* adjacent
neither *conj.* ni
nervous *adj.* nerveux
never *adv.* jamais
new *adj.* nouveau; neuf
next *adj.* prochain; *conj.* ensuite; ~ **to** *prep.*
    à côté de
nice *adj.* fin *qué.,* gentil
night *n.* nuit *f.*
nightclub *n.* boîte de nuit *f.,* discothèque *f.*
nightgown *n.* jaquette *f. qué.,* chemise de nuit *f.*
nimble *adj.* agile
no *adv.* non
noisy *adj.* bruyant
noon *n.* midi *m.*
nor *conj.* ni
north *n.* nord *m.*
North American *n.* nord-américain *m.*;
    adj. nord-américain
nose *n.* nez *m.*
note *n.* note *f.*; **(to)** *v.* noter, remarquer
notice (to) *v.* remarquer
now *adv.* maintenant, asteur *qué.*
nurse *n.* infirmière *f.*

O

obedient *adj.* obéissant
obey (to) *v.* obéir
oblige (to) *v.* obliger
observe (to) *v.* observer, remarquer
obtain (to) *v.* obtenir
occupy (to) *v.* occuper
of *prep.* de
offend (to) *v.* offenser
offer (to) *v.* offrir
official *adj.* officiel
often *adv.* souvent
oil *n.* huile *f.*
oily *adj.* huileux
old *adj.* âgé, vieux
omelet *n.* omelette *f.*
on *prep.* sur; en
onion *n.* oignon *m.*
open *adj.* ouvert; ~ (to) *v.* ouvrir
operate (to) *v.* opérer
oppose (to) *v.* opposer
or *conj.* ou
orange *n.* orange *f.*; *adj.* orange
orchestra *n.* orchestre *m.*
order (to) *v.* commander
oregano *n.* origan *m.*
organize (to) *v.* organiser
oriental *adj.* oriental
outing *n.* sortie *f.*
oven *n.* four *m.*
overalls *n.pl.* salopettes *f.pl. qué.*
overflow (to) *v.* déborder
owe (to) *v.* devoir
owl *n.* hibou *m.*
own (to) *v.* posséder

P

paint (to) *v.* peinturer *qué.*, peindre
pale *adj.* pâle
pan *n.* poêlon *m.*, poêlonne *f. qué.*
pancake *n.* crêpe *f.*
pants *n.pl.* pantalon *m.*
papaya *n.* papaye *f.*
paper *n.* papier *m.*
park *n.* parc *m.*; ~ (to) *v.* stationner, stationner (se)
parka *n.* parka *f.*, canadienne *f. qué.*
parking *n.* stationnement *m.*; ~ **meter** *n.*
      parcomètre *m.*
parsley *n.* persil *m.*
parsnip *n.* panais *m.*
pass (to) *v.* passer; dépasser (a car)
passive *adj.* passif
passport *n.* passeport *m.*
pasta *n.* pâtes *f.pl.*
patio *n.* patio *m. qué.*, terrasse *f.*
pay (to) *v.* payer
pea *n.* pois *m.*
peach *n.* pêche *f.*
pear *n.* poire *f.*
peel (to) *v.* peler; plemer (skin)
pen *n.* stylo *m.*, stylo-bille *m.*
pencil *n.* crayon *m.*
pepper *n.* piment *m. qué.*, poivron *m.* (vegetable);
      poivre *m.* (spice)
perceive (to) *v.* apercevoir
perfume *n.* parfum *m.*; ~ (to) *v.* parfumer
permit (to) *v.* permettre
perspire (to) *v.* transpirer
persuade (to) *v.* persuader
pharmaceutical *adj.* pharmaceutique
phone (to) *v.* téléphoner
physical *adj.* physique
physics *n.* physique *f.*

pie *n.* tarte *f.*; **meat ~** *n.* tourtière *f. qué.*;
    raisin ~ *n.* tarte à la farlouche *f. qué.*
piece *n.* morceau *m.*
pig *n.* cochon *m.*
pillow *n.* oreiller *m.*
pillowcase *n.* taie d'oreiller *f.*
pilot *n.* pilote *m.*; **~ (to)** *v.* piloter
pinch (to) *v.* pincer
pineapple *n.* ananas *m.*
pink *adj.* rose
pitch (to) *v.* lancer, pitcher *qué. slang*
place (to) *v.* placer
plan *n.* plan *m.*; **~ (to)** *v.* planifier
plant *n.* plante *f.*; **~ (to)** *v.* planter
plate *n.* assiette *f.*
plausible *adj.* plausible
play (to) *v.* jouer
pleasant *adj.* agréable
please (to) *v.* plaire
plum *n.* prune *f.*
pocket *n.* poche *f.*
pocketknife *n.* canif *m.*
pole *n.* poteau *m.*
polish (to) *v.* polir
pool *n.* piscine *f.*
poor *adj.* pauvre
popular *adj.* populaire; achalandé (establishment)
pork *n.* porc *m.*
Portuguese *n.* portugais *m.*; *adj.* portugais
possess (to) *v.* posséder
post *n.* poteau *m.*; **~ office** *n.* bureau de poste *m.*
postcard *n.* carte postale *f.*
pot *n.* chaudron *m. qué.*, casserole *f.*
potato *n.* patate *f. qué.*, pomme de terre *f.*
pour (to) *v.* verser
poutine *n.* poutine *f. qué.*
power *n.* pouvoir *m.*
practical *adj.* pratique
practice (to) *v.* pratiquer

precede (to) v. précéder
precise adj. précis
prefer (to) v. préférer
prepare (to) v. préparer
preposterous adj. absurde
prescription n. prescription f. qué., ordonnance f.
present n. cadeau m.; ~ (to) v. présenter
pretend (to) v. prétendre
pretentious adj. frais qué., prétentieux
prevent (to) v. prévenir
previous adj. précédent
price n. prix m.
pricey adj. cher
print (to) v. imprimer
private adj. privé
proceed (to) v. agir
produce (to) v. produire
prohibit (to) v. interdire
project n. projet m.
promise n. promesse f.; ~ (to) v. promettre
propose (to) v. proposer
protect (to) v. protéger
protest (to) v. protester
proud adj. fier
prove (to) v. prouver
provide (to) v. fournir
provoke (to) v. provoquer
psychology n. psychologie f.
public adj. public
publish (to) v. publier
puck n. poque f. qué., rondelle f.
pull (to) v. tirer; ~ out (to) v. arracher, retirer
punish (to) v. punir
purchase (to) v. acheter
purchased adj. acheté
purple adj. mauve
purse n. bourse f., sacoche f., sac à main m.
pursue (to) v. poursuivre

push (to) *v.* pousser
put (to) *v.* mettre; ~ **away (to)** *v.* serrer *qué.*;
    ~ **back (to)** *v.* remettre; ~ **out (to)**
    v. éteindre (fire)

Q

Quebecer *n.* québécois *m.*; *adj.* québécois
Québécois *n.* québécois *m.*; *adj.* québécois
question *n.* question *f.*; ~ **(to)** *v.* questionner
quiet *adj.* silencieux

R

rabbit *n.* lapin *m.*
raccoon *n.* raton-laveur *m.*; chat sauvage *m. qué.*
racquet *n.* raquette *f.*
radiator *n.* calorifère *m. qué.*; chauffrette *f. qué.*;
    radiateur *m.*
radio *n.* radio *f.*
radish *n.* radis *m.*
rag *n.* guénille *f. qué. inf.*, torchon *m.*
rain *n.* pluie *f.*; **freezing** ~ *n.* verglas *m.*; ~ **(to)**
    v. pleuvoir, mouiller *qué.*
rainy *adj.* pluvieux
raise (to) *v.* augmenter; hausser; lever
rare *adj.* rare
rarely *adv.* rarement
raspberry *n.* framboise *f.*
raw *adj.* cru
razor *n.* rasoir *m.*
reach (to) *v.* atteindre
read (to) *v.* lire
read *adj.* lu
realize (to) *v.* réaliser
reassure (to) *v.* rassurer
receive (to) *v.* recevoir

recent *adj.* récent
recipe *n.* recette *f.*
recite (to) *v.* réciter
recognize (to) *v.* reconnaître
recommend (to) *v.* recommander
recommended *adj.* recommandé
record (to) *v.* enregistrer
recover (to) *v.* guérir (illness); retrouver
     (find again)
red *adj.* rouge
redo (to) *v.* refaire
reduce (to) *v.* réduire
refrigerator *n.* frigidaire *m. qué.*, réfrigérateur *m.*
refuse (to) *v.* refuser
register (to) *v.* enregistrer
regret (to) *v.* regretter
reimburse (to) *v.* rembourser
reject (to) *v.* rejeter
relieved *adj.* soulagé
remember (to) *v.* souvenir (se)
remove (to) *v.* ôter, enlever
rent (to) *v.* louer
rented *adj.* loué
repair (to) *v.* réparer, arranger *inf.*
repeat (to) *v.* répéter
replace (to) *v.* remplacer
represent (to) *v.* représenter
reproach (to) *v.* reprocher
require (to) *v.* exiger
rescue (to) *v.* secourir
research (to) *v.* rechercher
reserve (to) *v.* réserver
reside (to) *v.* résider
resist (to) *v.* résister
resolve (to) *v.* résoudre
respect (to) *v.* respecter
rest (to) *v.* reposer (se) (oneself); reposer
restaurant *n.* restaurant *m.*
result *n.* résultat *m.*; ~ (to) *v.* résulter

retired *adj.* retraité
reunite (to) *v.* réunir
reveal (to) *v.* révéler
revise (to) *v.* réviser
rhyme (to) *v.* rimer
rich *adj.* riche
ridicule (to) *v.* ridiculiser
ridiculous *adj.* ridicule
right *n.* droite *f.* (direction)
ring (to) *v.* sonner
risk (to) *v.* risquer
roast *n.* rôti *m.*; ~ (to) *v.* rôtir
roasted *adj.* rôti
robe *n.* robe de chambre *f. qué.*, peignoir *m.*
rock *n.* roche *f.*; ~ (to) *v.* bercer
rocking chair *n.* chaise berçante *f. qué.*, berceuse *f.*
roll (to) *v.* rouler
roof *n.* toit *m.*
room *n.* pièce *f.*; chambre *f.*; salle *f.*
roommate *n.* côloc *m. qué.*, colocataire *m.*
rope *n.* corde *f.*
rose *n.* rose *f.*
rosemary *n.* romarin *m.*
rot (to) *v.* pourrir
row (to) *v.* ramer
rowboat *n.* chaloupe *f.*, barque *f.*
rowing *n.* aviron *m.*
rub (to) *v.* frotter
ruin (to) *v.* ruiner
run (to) *v.* courir; ~ away (to) *v.* fuir, enfuir (s')
Russian *n.* russe *m.*; *adj.* russe

S

sacred *adj.* sacré
sacrifice (to) *v.* sacrifier
sad *adj.* triste
safe *adj.* sauf, sûr

sail *n.* voile *f.*
sailing *n.* voile *f.*
sale *n.* vente *f.*, solde *m.*
salt *n.* sel *m.*; ~ **(to)** *v.* saler
salted *adj.* salé
salty *adj.* salé
salute **(to)** *v.* saluer
sand *n.* sable *m.*
sandal *n.* sandale *f.*
sandwich *n.* sandwich *m.*
sanitary *adj.* sanitaire
satisfy **(to)** *v.* satisfaire
sausage *n.* saucisse *f.*
save **(to)** *v.* sauver; économiser (time, money);
    épargner (money)
saw **(to)** *v.* scier
say **(to)** *v.* dire; ~ **again (to)** *v.* redire
scared *adj.* apeuré, effrayé
scarf *n.* foulard *m.*, écharpe *f.*
school *n.* école *f.*
science *n.* science *f.*
scratch **(to)** *v.* gratter
screen *n.* écran *m.*
seafood *n.* fruit de mer *m.*
seat *n.* siège *m.*
second *n.* seconde *f.*; *adj.* deuxième, second;
    ~ **from last** *adj.* avant-dernier
see **(to)** *v.* voir; ~ **again (to)** *v.* revoir
seem **(to)** *v.* sembler, paraître
seize **(to)** *v.* saisir
seldom *adv.* rarement
self-confident *adj.* sûr de soi
selfish *adj.* égoïste
sell **(to)** *v.* vendre
send **(to)** *v.* envoyer; ~ **back (to)** *v.* renvoyer
separate **(to)** *v.* séparer
separated *adj.* séparé
serve **(to)** *v.* servir
sew **(to)** *v.* coudre

shake (to) *v.* trembler; secouer; serrer (hand)

shampoo *n.* shampoing *m.*

share (to) *v.* partager

sharp *adj.* acéré, aigu, affilé

sharpen (to) *v.* aiguiser, affiler

sheep *n.* mouton *m.*

shelter *n.* abri *m.*; ~ **(to)** *v.* abriter

shine (to) *v.* briller, luire

shiny *adj.* luisant

shirt *n.* chemise *f.*

shiver (to) *v.* grelotter

shoe *n.* chaussure *f.*, soulier *m.*

shop *n.* boutique *f.*; ~ **(to)** *v.* magasiner *qué.*

shopping *n.* magasinage *m. qué.*; ~ **center** *n.* centre commercial *m.*, centre d'achat *m. qué.*

short *adj.* court, petit

shorts *n.pl.* shorts *f.pl.*

show *n.* spectacle *m.*, show *m. inf.*; ~ **(to)** *v.* montrer

shower *n.* douche *f.*

shrimp *n.* crevette *f.*

shuffle (to) *v.* brasser (playing cards)

sick *adj.* malade

sigh *n.* soupir *m.*; ~ **(to)** *v.* soupirer

sign (to) *v.* signer

signal (to) *v.* signaler

silent *adj.* silencieux

silver *n.* argent *m.*; *adj.* argent

since *prep.* depuis

sing (to) *v.* chanter; ~ **off-key (to)** *v.* fausser

single *adj.* célibataire

sink *n.* lavabo *m.* (bathroom), évier *m.* (kitchen); ~ **(to)** *v.* caler *qué.*; couler (boat)

sister *n.* soeur *f.*

sister-in-law *n.* belle-soeur *f.*

sit (to) *v.* asseoir (s'), assir (s') *qué.*

skate *n.* patin *m.*; ~ **(to)** *v.* patiner

skating *n.* patinage *m.*; **figure** ~ *n.* patinage artistique *m.*; **speed** ~ *n.* patinage de vitesse *m.*

skeptical *adj.* sceptique

ski *n.* ski *m.;* ~ **resort** *n.* centre de ski *m.;* ~ **(to)**
    v. skier

skiing *n.* ski *m.;* **downhill** ~ *n.* ski alpin *m.;*
    alpine ~ *n.* ski alpin *m.;* **cross-country** ~ *n.*
    ski de fond *m.*

skillful *adj.* adroit

skinny *adj.* maigre

skirt *n.* jupe *f.*

skunk *n.* bête puante *f. qué.,* mouffette *f.*

sky *n.* ciel *m.*

skyscraper *n.* gratte-ciel *m.*

slap *n.* claque *f.*

sleep (to) *v.* dormir

sleeping bag *n.* sac de couchage *m.*

slice (to) *v.* trancher

slide *n.* glissoire *f.;* **water** ~ *n.* glissade d'eau *f.;*
    ~ **(to)** *v.* glisser

slipper *n.* chaussette *f. qué.;* pantoufle *f.*

slow *adj.* lent

slush *n.* sloche *f. qué.*

smack *n.* claque *f.*

small *adj.* petit

smell (to) *v.* sentir

smile *n.* sourire *m.;* ~ **(to)** *v.* sourire

smoke *n.* boucane *f. qué.,* fumée *f.;* ~ **(to)** *v.* fumer

snack *n.* collation *f.;* ~ **(to)** *v.* grignoter

snail *n.* escargot *m.*

snobby *adj.* frais *qué.,* snob

snore (to) *v.* ronfler

snow *n.* neige *f.;* ~ **(to)** *v.* neiger

snowbank *n.* banc de neige *m. qué.,* congère *f.*

snowblower *n.* souffleuse *f. qué.*

snowboard *n.* planche à neige *f.,* snowboard *m.*

snowboarding *n.* snowboarding *m.*

snowpea *n.* pois mange-tout *m.*

snowshoes *n.pl.* raquettes *f.pl. qué.*

snowstorm *n.* tempête de neige *f.*

so *conj.* donc

soak (to) *v.* tremper; mouiller

soap *n.* savon *m.*

soccer *n.* soccer *m.*

sock *n.* bas *m.,* chaussette *f.*

soda *n.* liqueur *f. qué.*

sofa *n.* sofa *m. qué.,* divan *m.,* canapé *m.*

soft *adj.* doux

sold *adj.* vendu

solid *adj.* solide

solve (to) *v.* résoudre

son *n.* fils *m.*

song *n.* toune *f. qué. slang,* chanson *f.*

sophisticated *adj.* sophistiqué

sort (to) *v.* trier

sour *adj.* aigre, sur

south *n.* sud *m.*

South African *n.* sud-africain *m.;*
    adj. sud-africain

South American *n.* sud-américain *m.;*
    adj. sud-américain

souvenir *n.* souvenir *m.*

Spanish *n.* espagnol *m.; adj.* espagnol

speed *n.* vitesse *f.;* ~ (to) *v.* flyer *qué. slang*

spend (to) *v.* dépenser (money)

spice *n.* épice *f.*

spicy *adj.* épicé; piquant

spinach *n.* épinard *m.*

spit (to) *v.* cracher

spoken *adj.* parlé

spoon *n.* cuillère *f.*

sprawl out (to) *v.* effoirer (s') *qué. slang,* étaler
    (s')

spring *n.* printemps *m.* (season)

squash *n.* courge *f.,* gourde *f.* (vegetable); squash
    m. (sport)

squeeze (to) *v.* serrer

squirrel *n.* écureuil *m.*

stain *n.* tache *f.;* ~ (to) *v.* tacher

stamp *n.* timbre *m.*
star *n.* étoile *f.*
start (to) *v.* commencer
stay (to) *v.* demeurer, rester; ~ **up late (to)**
    v. veiller
steak *n.* steak *m.*
steal (to) *v.* voler, piquer *inf.*
sticky *adj.* collant
sting (to) *v.* piquer
stitch (to) *v.* coudre
stop (to) *v.* arrêter
store *n.* magasin *m.*
storm *n.* tempête *f.*
story *n.* histoire *f.*
straight *adj.* droit, drette *qué. slang; adv.* droit
strange *adj.* étrange
strawberry *n.* fraise *f.*
street *n.* rue *f.*
striped *adj.* rayé
strong *adj.* fort
struggle *n.* lutte *f.*
stubborn *adj.* têtu, entêté
student *n.* étudiant *m.*
study (to) *v.* étudier
stupid *adj.* twitte *qué.*, stupide
submit (to) *v.* soumettre
subtract (to) *v.* soustraire
succeed (to) *v.* réussir
sue (to) *v.* poursuivre
suffer (to) *v.* souffrir
sufficient *adj.* suffisant
sugar *n.* sucre *m.*; ~ **shack** *n.* cabane à sucre *f. qué.*
suggest (to) *v.* suggérer
suit *n.* complet *m.* (for men)
suitcase *n.* valise *f.*
sulk (to) *v.* bouder
summer *n.* été *m.*; **Indian** ~ *n.* été des Indiens
    m., été indien *m. qué.*

sun *n.* soleil *m.*

sunbathe (to) *v.* griller (se faire) *qué.*, bronzer (se faire)

sunny *adj.* ensoleillé

sunscreen *n.* crème solaire *f.*, écran solaire *m.*

supervise (to) *v.* surveiller, diriger

supper *n.* souper *m.*

supply (to) *v.* fournir

support (to) *v.* appuyer; soutenir

surgery *n.* chirurgie *f.*

surprise (to) *v.* surprendre

surprised *adj.* surpris

surround (to) *v.* entourer

survive (to) *v.* survivre

suspicious *adj.* suspect

swallow (to) *v.* envaler *qué.*, avaler

swear (to) *v.* sacrer *qué.* (obscenity); jurer

sweater *n.* chandail *m.*

sweep (to) *v.* balayer

sweet *adj.* sucré

sweet-and-sour *adj.* aigre-doux

sweetened *adj.* sucré

swim (to) *v.* baigner (se); nager

swimming *n.* natation *f.*

swimsuit *n.* costume de bain *m. qué.*, maillot de bain *m.*

Swiss *n.* suisse *m.; adj.* suisse

switch *n.* switch *f. qué.*, interrupteur *m.*

syrup *n.* sirop *m.;* **cough ~** *n.* sirop pour la toux *m.;* **maple ~** *n.* sirop d'érable *m.*

T

table *n.* table *f.*

tablespoon *n.* cuillère à table *f. qué.*, cuillère à soupe *f.*

tacky *adj.* quétaine *qué.*

take (to) *v.* prendre; ~ **away (to)** *v.* ôter; ~ **care of (to)** *v.* occuper (s'); ~ **off (to)** *v.* enlever, ôter (something); décoller (airplane)

talk (to) *v.* parler, causer

tall *adj.* grand

tart *adj.* aigre

taste (to) *v.* goûter

taxi *n.* taxi *m.*

T-bar *n.* T-bar *m. qué.*, remonte-pente *m.*

tea *n.* thé *m.*

teabag *n.* poche de thé *f. qué.*, sachet de thé *m.*

teach (to) *v.* enseigner; instruire

tear (to) *v.* déchirer; ~ **out (to)** *v.* arracher

teaspoon *n.* cuillère à thé *f. qué.*

technical *adj.* technique

technological *adj.* technologique

telephone *n.* téléphone *m.*

television *n.* télévision *f.*

tell (to) *v.* dire; raconter; ~ **again (to)** *v.* redire

tempt (to) *v.* tenter

tender *adj.* tendre

tennis *n.* tennis *m.*

tent *n.* tente *f.*

terrace *n.* terrasse *f.*

thank (to) *v.* remercier

theater *n.* théâtre *m.*

theft *n.* vol *m.*

then *conj.* puis

thick *adj.* épais

thin *adj.* mince

thing *n.* chose *f.*, cossin *m. qué. inf.*, gugusse *f. qué. inf.*, patente *f. qué. inf.*

think (to) *v.* penser; ~ **over (to)** *v.* réfléchir

third *adj.* troisième

thirsty *adj.* assoiffé

thorough *adj.* approfondi

through *prep.* à travers

throw (to) *v.* lancer, garrocher *qué. slang;* ~ **away**
    (to) *v.* jeter
thumb *n.* pouce *m.*
thunderstorm *n.* orage *m.*
thyme *n.* thym *m.*
ticket *n.* billet *m.*
tighten (to) *v.* serrer
tilt (to) *v.* pencher
time *n.* temps *m.*
timid *adj.* gêné
tired *adj.* fatigué
tissue *n.* mouchoir *m.*
to *prep.* à; en
toast *n.* rôtie *f.*
today *adv.* aujourd'hui
toe *n.* orteil *m.*
toilet *n.* toilette *f.*
tomato *n.* tomate *f.*
tongue *n.* langue *f.*
tonight *adv.* ce soir
toothbrush *n.* brosse à dents *f.*
toothpaste *n.* dentifrice m.
total *adj.* total
touch (to) *v.* toucher
toward *prep.* vers
toy *n.* jouet *m.*, bébelle *f. qué. inf.*
track and field *n.* athlétisme *m.*
train *n.* train *m.;* ~ **station** *n.* gare *f.;* ~ **(to)**
    v. entraîner
traitor *n.* vendu *m. qué.*, traitre *m.*
transform (to) *v.* transformer
translate (to) *v.* traduire
translation *n.* traduction *f.*
transport (to) *v.* transporter
travel (to) *v.* voyager
travel agent *n.* agent de voyage *m.*
tree *n.* arbre *m.*
tremble (to) *v.* trembler
triathlon *n.* triathlon *m.*
trouble *n.* trouble *m.*

true *adj.* vrai

trunk *n.* valise *f. qué.* (car), coffre arrière *m.* (car)

try (to) *v.* tenter, essayer; ~ **on (to)** *v.* essayer

tune *n.* toune *f. qué.*

tuque *n.* tuque *f.*

turkey *n.* dinde *f.*

turn (to) *v.* virer *qué.*, tourner; ~ **on (to)** *v.* allumer (tv, light)

turnip *n.* navet *m.*

turquoise *adj.* turquoise

U

ugly *adj.* laid

uncle *n.* oncle *m.*, mononcle *m. qué. inf.*

under *prep.* sous

understand (to) *v.* comprendre

underwear *n.* bobettes *f.pl. qué. inf.*, caleçons *m.pl.*, sous-vêtement *m.*

undo (to) *v.* défaire

undress (to) *v.* déshabiller (se) (oneself)

uneasy *adj.* anxieux

unhappy *adj.* malheureux

unimaginable *adj.* inimaginable

unique *adj.* unique

unite (to) *v.* unir, joindre

United States *n.* États-Unis *m.pl.*

university *n.* université *f.*

unlock (to) *v.* débarrer *qué.*, déverrouiller

unlocked *adj.* débarré *qué.*, déverrouillé

unofficial *adj.* officieux

until *prep.* jusqu'à

urban *adj.* urbain

urgent *adj.* urgent

use (to) *v.* utiliser; employer; ~ **up (to)** *v.* épuiser

used *adj.* usé, magané *qué. slang*

utensil *n.* ustensile *m. qué.*

V

vacuum cleaner *n.* balayeuse *f. qué.*, aspirateur *m.*
valid *adj.* valide
van *n.* vanne *f. qué.*, fourgonnette *f.*
vary (to) *v.* varier
VCR *n.* magnétoscope *m.*
vegetarian *n.* végétarien *m.; adj.* végétarien
veil *n.* voile *m.*
verify (to) *v.* vérifier
Vietnamese *n.* vietnamien *m.; adj.* vietnamien
vinegar *n.* vinaigre *m.*
visa *n.* visa *m.*
visit *n.* visite *f.;* ~ **(to)** *v.* visiter
visual *adj.* visuel
volleyball *n.* volleyball *m.*
vomit (to) *v.* dégueuler *qué. slang,* vomir
vote (to) *v.* voter

W

waffle *n.* gaufre *f.*
wait (to) *v.* attendre
wake (to) *v.* éveiller, réveiller; éveiller (s'),
    réveiller (se) (oneself)
walk *n.* marche *f.;* ~ **(to)** *v.* marcher
wall *n.* mur *m.*
wallet *n.* portefeuille *m.*
want (to) *v.* vouloir
warm *adj.* chaud
warn (to) *v.* avertir, prévenir
wash (to) *v.* laver
washcloth *n.* débarbouillette *f. qué.*
watch *n.* montre *f.;* ~ **(to)** *v.* regarder; ~ **over (to)**
    v. surveiller
water *n.* eau *f.;* ~ **fountain** *n.* abreuvoir *m. qué.,*
    fontaine *f.;* **spring** ~ *n.* eau de source *f.;*
    ~ **(to)** *v.* arroser

watermelon *n.* melon d'eau *m. qué.*, pastèque *f.*
wear (to) *v.* porter (clothes)
wed (to) *v.* épouser, marier
week *n.* semaine *f.*
weekend *n.* fin de semaine *f.*, week-end *m.*
weekly *adj.* hebdomadaire
weigh (to) *v.* peser
weight *n.* poids *m.*; **gain ~ (to)** *v.* engraisser; **lose**
    ~ (to) *v.* maigrir
welcome *n.* bienvenue *f.*; **~ (to)** *v.* accueillir
welcoming *adj.* accueillant
west *n.* ouest *m.*
western *adj.* occidental
wet (to) *v.* mouiller
what *pron.* quoi
when *adv.* quand; *conj.* quand
where *adv.* où; *conj.* où
while *prep.* pendant
whine (to) *v.* chialer *qué.*
whiner *n.* chialeux *m. qué.*
whirlpool *n.* bain tourbillon *m. qué.*, bain à
    remous *m.*
whistle (to) *v.* siffler
white *adj.* blanc
who *pron.* qui
why *adv.* pourquoi; *conj.* pourquoi
win (to) *v.* gagner
wind *n.* vent *m.*
window *n.* fenêtre *f.*
wine *n.* vin *m.*
winter *n.* hiver *m.*
wipe (to) *v.* essuyer
wish (to) *v.* désirer, souhaiter, espérer
with *prep.* avec
without *prep.* sans
wolf *n.* loup *m.*
wonderful *adj.* merveilleux
woodchuck *n.* siffleux *m. qué.*, marmotte *f.*
work *n.* job *f. qué.*, travail *m.*; **~ (to)** *v.* travailler

worried *adj.* inquiet
wrap (to) *v.* envelopper, emballer
wrestling *n.* lutte *f.*
wrinkle *n.* ride *f.*
wrinkled *adj.* ridé
write (to) *v.* écrire
written *adj.* écrit

Y

yawn (to) *v.* bâiller
yell (to) *v.* crier
yellow *adj.* jaune
yes *adv.* oui
young *adj.* jeune
Yule log *n.* bûche de Noël *f. qué.*

Z

zip (to) *v.* zipper *qué.*
zipper *n.* fermeture éclair *f.*, fermoir *m.*, zipper
       m. qué. inf.
zucchini *n.* zucchini *m. qué.*, courgette *f.*

QUÉBÉCOIS PHRASEBOOK

USEFUL EXPRESSIONS

GREETINGS

Hello.
  Allo.
  Salut.
  Bonjour.

Good morning.
  Bonjour.

Good afternoon.
  Bonjour.

Good evening.
  Bonsoir.

Good night.
  Bonne nuit.

FAREWELLS

Goodbye.
  Au revoir.

See you soon.
  À bientôt.

See you later.
  À plus tard.

See you next time.
  À la prochaine.

See you tomorrow.
  À demain.

See you tonight.
À ce soir.

ETIQUETTE

Nice to meet you.
Enchanté.

How are you?
Comment allez-vous?
Comment ça va?

Fine, and you?
Bien, et vous?

Not well.
Mal.

So-so.
Comme ci, comme ça.

Welcome.
Bienvenue.

Please.
S'il vous plaît.

Thank you.
Merci.

You're welcome.
De rien.
Avec plaisir.

Bon voyage!
Bon voyage!

Have a nice day.
Bonne journée.

Excuse me.
Excusez-moi.

USEFUL EXPRESSIONS

Yes.
Oui.

No.
Non.

Okay.
D'accord.

I'm sorry.
Je suis désolé.

I don't understand.
Je ne comprends pas.

I understand.
Je comprends.

Do you understand?
Est-ce que vous comprenez?

I do not speak French.
Je ne parle pas français.

Do you speak English?
Parlez-vous anglais?

Can you help me?
Pouvez-vous m'aider?

Can you tell me what this means?
Pouvez-vous me dire ce que cela signifie?

Speak slower please.
Parlez plus lentement s'il vous plaît.

Please repeat.
Pourriez-vous répéter?

How do you say ... in French?
Comment dit-on ... en français?

I am lost.
Je suis perdu.

Where is ...?
Où est ...?

Wait!
Attendez!

I like ...
J'aime ...

I don't like ...
Je n'aime pas ...

Do you have any change?
Avez-vous de la monnaie?

How long will it take?
Combien de temps cela prendra-t-il?

How much does it cost?
Combien ça coûte?

What is the problem?
Quel est le problème?

USEFUL EXPRESSIONS

What is it?
Qu'est-ce que c'est?

What time do you close?
À quelle heure fermez-vous?

What is the admission fee?
Combien coûte l'entrée?

Can I take pictures?
Puis-je prendre des photos?

Is there a guided tour?
Y a-t-il une visite guidée?

QUESTION WORDS

Who?
Qui?

What?
Quoi?

When?
Quand?

Why?
Pourquoi?

Where?
Où?

How?
Comment?

INTRODUCTIONS

What's your name?
Comment vous appelez-vous?

My name is ...
Je m'appelle ...

What is his/her name?
Comment s'appelle-t-il/-t-elle?

His/her name is ...
Il/elle s'appelle ...

Mr., Sir
Monsieur

Mrs.
Madame

Miss
Mademoiselle

NATIONALITY

Where are you from?
D'où venez-vous?

I'm from ...	**Je viens ...**
...Australia.	**...d'Australie.**
...Brazil.	**...du Brésil.**
...Canada.	**...du Canada.**
...China.	**...de la Chine.**
...England.	**...d'Angleterre.**
...Germany.	**...d'Allemagne.**
...Ireland.	**...d'Irlande.**
...Italy.	**...d'Italie.**

...Japan.	...du Japon.
...Korea.	...de Corée.
...Mexico.	...du Mexique.
...the Netherlands.	...des Pays-Bas.
...New Zealand.	...de Nouvelle-Zélande.
...Portugal.	...du Portugal.
...Scotland.	...d'Écosse.
...South Africa.	...d'Afrique du Sud.
...Spain.	...d'Espagne.
...Switzerland.	...de la Suisse.
...the United States.	...des États-Unis.

I'm ...	Je suis ...
...American.	...américain.
...Australian.	...australien.
...Brazilian.	...brésilien.
...British.	...britannique.
...Canadian.	...canadien.
...Chinese.	...chinois.
...Dutch.	...néerlandais.
...German.	...allemand.
...Irish.	...irlandais.
...Italian.	...italien.
...Japanese.	...japonais.
...Korean.	...coréen.
...Mexican.	...mexicain.
...New Zealander.	...néo-zélandais.
...Portuguese.	...portugais.
...Scotland.	...écossais.
...South African.	...sud-africain.
...Spanish.	...espagnol.
...Swiss.	...suisse.

AGE

How old are you?
Quel âge avez-vous?

I am ... years old.
J'ai ... ans.

When is your birthday?
Quelle est votre date de fête?
Quelle est votre date d'anniversaire?

FAMILY

Are you married?
Êtes-vous marié?

I am married.
Je suis marié.

I am single.
Je suis célibataire.

Do you have a ...   **Avez-vous ...**
...boyfriend?   **...un copain?**
...girlfriend?   **...une copine?**

How many children do you have?
Combien d'enfants avez-vous?

I don't have children.
Je n'ai pas d'enfants.

How many brothers and sisters do you have?
Combien de frères et de soeurs avez-vous?

OCCUPATIONS

What do you do for a living?
Que faites-vous dans la vie?

INTRODUCTIONS

I am ...	Je suis ...
...an accountant.	...comptable.
...a businessman/ businesswoman.	...homme/ femme d'affaires.
...a dentist.	...dentiste.
...a diplomat.	...diplomate.
...a doctor.	...médecin.
...an economist.	...économiste.
...an engineer.	...ingénieur.
...a farmer.	...agriculteur/ fermier.
...a flight attendant.	...agent de bord.
...a journalist.	...journaliste.
...a lawyer.	...avocat.
...a mechanic.	...mécanicien.
...a nurse.	...infirmière/ infirmier.
...a pilot.	...pilote.
...a scientist.	...scientifique.
...a secretary.	...secrétaire.
...a soldier.	...soldat.
...a student.	...étudiant.
...a teacher.	...professeur.
...a translator.	...traducteur.
...a writer.	...écrivain.

Where do you work?
Où travaillez-vous?

UPON YOUR ARRIVAL

AT THE AIRPORT

Where is the information booth?
Où est le bureau des renseignements?

I have lost my ticket.
J'ai perdu mon billet.

I have lost my boarding pass.
J'ai perdu ma carte d'embarquement.

I have lost my luggage.
J'ai perdu mes bagages.

These bags are not mine.
Ces sacs ne sont pas à moi.

My suitcase was damaged.
Ma valise a été endommagée.

Where can I find luggage carts?
Où sont les chariots à bagage?

Where do I get the connecting flight to ...?
**Où dois-je prendre la correspondance
    pour ...?**

I have missed my flight/my connection.
J'ai manqué mon vol/ma correspondance.

Can I upgrade to first class?
**Puis-je changer mon billet pour une
    première classe?**

Can I check my bags?
Puis-je enregistrer mes bagages?

I am looking for gate number ...
Je cherche la porte d'embarquement ...

Flight number ... to ...
Le vol ... à destination de ...

Canceled
Annulé

Delayed
Retardé

CUSTOMS

Your passport please.
Votre passeport, s'il vous plaît.

What is your nationality?
De quelle nationalité êtes-vous?
Quelle est votre nationalité?

My name is ...
Je m'appelle ...

Do you have anything to declare?
Avez-vous quelque chose à déclarer?

I have nothing to declare.
Je n'ai rien à déclarer.

What is the purpose of your stay?
Raison de votre séjour?

Vacation
Vacances

Business trip
Voyage d'affaires

How long will you be staying in Quebec?
Combien de temps durera votre séjour au Québec?

SERVICES

Where can I rent a car?
Où puis-je louer une voiture?

Where is the duty-free shop?
Où est le magasin hors-taxe?

Where can I get the bus for downtown?
Où est l'autobus pour le centre-ville?

Where are the taxis?
Où sont les taxis?

Where can I exchange money?
Où puis-je changer mon argent?

Where can I cash traveler's checks?
Où puis-je changer des chèques de voyage?

Where can I find an ATM machine?
Où puis-je trouver un guichet automatique?

Where are the restrooms?
Où sont les toilettes?

ACCOMMODATIONS

Hotel
Hôtel

Motel
Motel

Bed & Breakfast
Bed and Breakfast
Café et Couette

Youth Hostel
Auberge de jeunesse

Campground
Terrain de camping

CHECKING IN

I have a reservation.
J'ai une réservation.

I would like a room ...	**Je voudrais une chambre ...**
...for one night.	**...pour une nuit.**
...for the weekend.	**...pour la fin de semaine.**
...for a week.	**...pour une semaine.**
...with a single bed.	**...avec un lit simple.**
...with a double bed.	**...avec un lit double.**

How much is it?
Combien ça coûte?

Does the price include ...	**Est-ce que le prix comprend ...**
...taxes?	**...les taxes?**
...service?	**...le service?**
...breakfast?	**...le déjeuner?**

Could you have my luggage sent to my room please?
> **Pourriez-vous faire monter mes bagages, s'il vous plaît?**

Can we have adjoining rooms?
> **Pouvons-nous avoir des chambres attenantes?**

Are there supervised activities for children?
> **Y a-t-il des activités surveillées pour les enfants?**

Is there ...	**Y a-t-il ...**
...a hair dryer?	**...un sèche-cheveux?**
...a television?	**...une télévision?**
...a minibar?	**...un minibar?**
...air conditioning?	**...l'air climatisé?**
...a sauna?	**...un sauna?**
...a swimming pool?	**...une piscine?**
...a laundry service?	**...un service de blanchisserie?**
...parking?	**...un stationnement?**

SERVICES

Can you fill the minibar, please?
> **Pourriez-vous remplir le minibar, s'il vous plaît?**

Can you wake me at ... please?
Pouvez-vous me réveiller à ... s'il vous plaît?

Can I have ...	Puis-je avoir ...
...an ashtray?	...un cendrier?
...another blanket?	...une autre couverture?
...another pillow?	...un autre oreiller?
...some coat hangers?	...des cintres?
...some soap?	...du savon?
...a few towels?	...des serviettes?
...a few facecloths?	...des débarbouillettes?
...some toilet paper?	...du papier de toilette?
...some shampoo?	...du shampoing?
...some conditioner?	...du revitalisant?

Please charge this to my room.
Mettez cela sur ma note, s'il vous plaît.

PROBLEMS AT THE HOTEL

May I speak to the manager?
Puis-je parler au directeur?

My window is stuck.
Ma fenêtre est coincée.

The air conditioning is not working.
Le climatiseur ne fonctionne pas.

The room is dirty.
La chambre est sale.

The heater is not working.
Le chauffage ne fonctionne pas.

The room is too noisy.
La chambre est trop bruyante.

The toilet is clogged.
La toilette est bouchée.

CHECKING OUT

At what time do we have to check out?
À quelle heure faut-il libérer la chambre?

Could you keep our luggage until ...?
Pouvez-vous garder nos bagages jusqu'à ...?

I would like to stay an extra night.
J'aimerais rester une nuit de plus.

I will be leaving tomorrow.
Je pars demain.

Could you bring my luggage downstairs please?
Pourriez-vous descendre mes bagages, s'il vous plaît?

Could you prepare my bill please?
Pourriez-vous préparer ma note, s'il vous plaît?

Could you call me a taxi please?
Pourriez-vous m'appeler un taxi, s'il vous plaît?

GETTING AROUND

Where is the ...	Où est ...
...bus station?	...le terminus d'autobus?
...nearest bus stop?	...l'arrêt d'autobus le plus près?
...port?	...le port?
...train station?	...la gare?
...nearest subway station?	...la station de métro la plus près?

What time does the ... leave?	À quelle heure part ...
...boat...	...le bateau?
...bus...	...l'autobus?
...plane...	...l'avion?
...train...	...le train?

I want to go to ...
Je veux aller à/au ...

Could you tell me how to get to ...?
Pourriez-vous me dire comment me rendre à/au ...?

Is it far from here?
Est-ce que c'est loin d'ici?

Can I walk there?
Je peux y aller à pied?

Can you show me on this map?
Pourriez-vous me le montrer sur cette carte?

What street is this?
Quelle est cette rue?

How long does it take to get to ...?
Combien de temps est-ce que ça prend pour aller ...?

DIRECTIONS

Straight ahead
Tout droit

Turn right/left ...   **Tournez à droite/gauche ...**

...at the next corner.   **...à la prochaine intersection.**

...at the next traffic lights.   **...à la prochaine lumière.**

Where does this road go?
Où cette route mène-t-elle?

What is the best route to ...?
Quelle est la meilleure route pour aller à/au ...?

Near
Près

Next to
À côté de

Behind
Derrière

In front of
Devant

North
Nord

GETTING AROUND

South
Sud

West
Ouest

East
Est

GETTING AROUND BY TAXI

Where can I get a taxi?
Où pourrais-je trouver un taxi?

Please take me to this address.
**Conduisez-moi à cette adresse, s'il
vous plaît.**

How much is it per kilometer?
C'est combien le kilomètre?

Please wait here for a few minutes.
**Attendez-moi quelques minutes, s'il
vous plaît.**

You can drop me off here.
Vous pouvez me déposer ici.

Stop at the corner, please.
Arrêtez-vous au coin, s'il vous plaît.

Take me to the airport/train station, please.
**Amenez-moi à l'aéroport/la gare, s'il
vous plaît.**

I am in a hurry.
Je suis pressé.

Keep the change.
Gardez la monnaie.

GETTING AROUND BY BUS

Does this bus go to ...?
Cet autobus se rend-il à/au ...?

What is the fare?
Combien ça coûte?

When is the last bus?
À quelle heure part le dernier autobus?

Where do I take the bus for ...?
Où puis-je prendre l'autobus pour ...?

Which bus do I take to go to ...?
**Quel autobus dois-je prendre pour aller
  à/au ...?**

Please tell me when to get off the bus.
**Dites-moi où je dois descendre, s'il
  vous plaît.**

Is this seat taken?
Cette place est-elle libre?

GETTING AROUND BY TRAIN

When is the next train to ...?
**À quelle heure part le prochain train
  pour ...?**

Where can I buy a ticket?
Où puis-je acheter un billet?

I would like a round-trip ticket to ...
Je voudrais un billet aller-retour pour ...

I would like a one-way ticket to ...
Je voudrais un aller simple pour ...

Where are the luggage lockers?
Où est la consigne automatique?

Is there a discount for children?
Y a-t-il une réduction pour les enfants?

What time does the train leave?
À quelle heure part le train?

What time is the last train?
À quelle heure part le dernier train?

Is this the train to ...?
C'est bien le train pour ...?

What time do we get to ...?
À quelle heure arrivons-nous à ...?

Does this train stop at ...?
Ce train s'arrête-t-il à ...?

Are we on time?
Sommes-nous à l'heure?

Is this seat taken?
Cette place est-elle libre?

RENTING A CAR

I would like to rent a car.
J'aimerais louer une voiture.

automatic transmission
transmission automatique

manual transmission
transmission manuelle

Do I pay in advance?
Dois-je payer à l'avance?

Do I have to pay a deposit?
Dois-je laisser un dépôt?

Is tax included?
La taxe est-elle comprise?

Do I have to return the car here?
Dois-je rapporter la voiture ici?

I would like to leave the car at the airport.
Je voudrais laisser la voiture à l'aéroport.

CAR TALK

What is the speed limit?
Quelle est la limite de vitesse?

Can I park here?
Puis-je me stationner ici?

What time does the parking lot close?
À quelle heure le terrain de stationnement ferme-t-il?

Fill the tank please.
Le plein, s'il vous plaît.

Can you check the oil?
Pouvez-vous vérifier l'huile?

Can you send a tow truck?
Pouvez-vous envoyer une dépanneuse/une remorqueuse?

Can you take me to the nearest garage?
Pouvez-vous me conduire au garage le plus près?

I have a flat tire.
J'ai une crevaison.

My car has broken down.
Ma voiture est en panne.

The battery is dead.
Ma batterie est à plat.

The engine is overheating.
Mon moteur chauffe.

There has been an accident.
Il y a eu un accident.

DINING OUT

I'm looking for ... restaurant.
Je cherche un restaurant ...
...a Chinese...
...chinois.
...a fast-food...
...de fast-food/ de restauration rapide.
...a French...
...français.
...an Indian...
...indien.
...an Italian...
...italien.
...a Japanese...
...japonais.
...a Mexican...
...mexicain.
...a sushi...
...de sushi.
...a Thai...
...thaïlandais.
...a vegetarian...
...végétarien.
...a Vietnamese...
...vietnamien.

I would like to reserve a table for ...
J'aimerais réserver une table pour ...

I have a reservation.
J'ai une réservation.

Table for ... please.
Une table pour ... personnes, s'il vous plaît.

Smoking/non-smoking
Fumeur/non-fumeur

Do you have a specialty?
Avez-vous une spécialité?

Do you have a kids' menu?
Avez-vous un menu pour enfants?

DINING OUT

Can I see the wine list?
Je peux voir la liste des vins?

A bottle of white/red wine please.
Une bouteille de vin blanc/rouge, s'il vous plaît.

Can I see the dessert menu?
Je peux voir la carte des desserts?

I would like my steak ... J'aimerais mon steak ...
...very rare.	...bleu.
...rare.	...saignant.
...medium rare.	...cuit à point.
...well done.	...bien cuit.

COMPLAINTS AND COMPLIMENTS

This is cold.
C'est froid.

This is not what I ordered.
Ce n'est pas ce que j'ai commandé.

This is excellent.
C'est excellent.

FOOD AND DRINK

apple	**pomme**
apricot	**abricot**
artichoke	**artichaut**
asparagus	**asperge**
avocado	**avocat**
bacon	**bacon**
bagel	**bagel**
banana	**banane**

beer	**bière**
beet	**betterave**
black currant	**cassis**
bread	**pain**
Brussels sprouts	**choux de Bruxelles**
butter	**beurre**
cabbage	**chou**
cake	**gâteau**
carrot	**carotte**
cauliflower	**chou-fleur**
celery	**céleri**
cereal	**céréales**
cheese	**fromage**
cherry	**cerise**
chicken	**poulet**
chicken wings	**ailes de poulet**
chocolate	**chocolat**
club sandwich	**club sandwich**
coffee	**café**
corn	**maïs, blé d'Inde**
corn dog	**pogo**
croissant	**croissant**
cucumber	**concombre**
date	**datte**
doughnut	**beigne**
egg	**œuf**
eggplant	**aubergine**
fish	**poisson**
French fries	**patates frites**
garlic	**ail**
gherkin	**cornichon**
grape	**raisin**
grapefruit	**pamplemousse**
guava	**goyave**
ham	**jambon**
hamburger	**hamburger**
herbal tea	**tisane**
honey	**miel**
hot chocolate	**chocolat chaud**

hot dog	**hot-dog**
ice cream	**crème glacée**
jam	**confiture**
juice	**jus**
ketchup	**ketchup**
leek	**poireau**
lemon	**citron**
lettuce	**laitue**
lime	**lime**
mango	**mangue**
maple syrup	**sirop d'érable**
melon	**melon**
milk	**lait**
muffin	**muffin**
mushroom	**champignon**
mustard	**moutarde**
olive	**olive**
onion	**oignon**
onion rings	**rondelles d'oignon**
orange	**orange**
pancake	**crêpe**
passion fruit	**fruit de la passion**
peach	**pêche**
peanut butter	**beurre d'arachides**
pear	**poire**
pepper	**piment, poivron**
pickle	**cornichon**
pie	**tarte**
pineapple	**ananas**
pizza	**pizza**
plum	**prune**
pork	**porc**
potato	**patate, pomme de terre**
poutine*	**poutine**
radish	**radis**
raisin	**raisin sec**
raspberry	**framboise**

*Poutine = French fries with cheese curds and gravy

relish	**relish**
ribs	**côtes levées**
rice	**riz**
roast beef	**rôti de boeuf**
salad	**salade**
salsa	**salsa**
sausage	**saucisse**
shallot	**échalotte**
soft drink	**liqueur**
soup	**soupe**
spinach	**épinard**
squash	**courge**
steak	**steak**
strawberry	**fraise**
tea	**thé**
tomato	**tomate**
turkey	**dinde**
turnip	**navet**
veal	**veau**
water	**eau**
watermelon	**melon d'eau**
wine	**vin**
zucchini	**courgette, zucchini**

SHOPPING

I am just looking.
Je ne fais que regarder.

Is this all you have?
Est-ce tout ce que vous avez?

I am looking for a souvenir.
Je cherche un souvenir.

I will take this one.
Je vais prendre celui-là/celle-là.

Where is the cash register?
Où est la caisse?

What is your return policy?
Quelle est votre politique de retour?

Can I exchange this, please?
Puis-je échanger ceci, s'il vous plaît?

CLOTHING STORE

I'm looking for ...	Je cherche ...
...a belt.	...une ceinture.
...a blouse.	...une blouse.
...boots.	...des bottes.
...a bra.	...un soutien-gorge, une brassière.
...a coat.	...un manteau.
...a dress.	...une robe.
...gloves.	...des gants.
...a hat.	...un chapeau.
...jeans.	...des jeans.

...a nightgown.	...une jaquette.
...pants.	...un pantalon.
...pantyhose.	...des bas de nylon.
...pyjamas.	...un pyjama.
...a raincoat.	...un imperméable.
...a shirt.	...une chemise.
...shoes.	...des souliers.
...shorts.	...des shorts.
...a skirt.	...une jupe.
...socks.	...des bas.
...a swimsuit.	...un maillot/ costume de bain.
...a tie.	...une cravate.
...a T-shirt.	...un T-shirt.
...underwear.	...des sous- vêtements.

Can I try this on?
Est-ce que je peux l'essayer?

Can I have this in a bigger/smaller size?
Est-ce que je peux avoir une taille plus grande/plus petite?

Can I exchange it if it does not fit?
Puis-je l'échanger si ça ne fait pas?

Do you have this in other colors?
Avez-vous ceci dans d'autres couleurs?

Is it dry-clean only?
Faut-il le nettoyer à sec seulement?

Is it machine washable?
Est-ce lavable à la machine?

Will it shrink?
Est-ce que ça rétrécit?

SHOPPING

FABRICS & PATTERNS

acrylic	**acrylique**
angora	**angora**
cashmere	**cachemire**
corduroy	**corduroy**
cotton	**coton**
denim	**denim**
fur	**fourrure**
knitted	**tricot**
lace	**dentelle**
leather	**cuir**
linen	**lin**
long sleeve	**manche longue**
lycra	**lycra**
nylon	**nylon**
plaid	**écossais, à carreaux**
polk-a-dot	**à pois**
polyester	**polyester**
rayon	**rayonne**
satin	**satin**
short sleeve	**manche courte**
silk	**soie**
striped	**rayé**
suede	**suède**
velvet	**velours**
wool	**laine**

BOOKSTORE

I am looking for a book by ...
Je cherche un livre écrit par ...

Has this book been translated into English?
Est-ce que ce livre a été traduit en anglais?

Where are the ...	Où sont les ...
...science fiction novels?	...livres de science-fiction?
...romance novels?	...romans d'amour?
...detective novels?	...romans policiers?
...spy novels?	...romans d'espionnage?
...comic books?	...bandes dessinées?
...travel guides?	...guides de voyages?
...magazines?	...revues?
...cookbooks?	...livres de recettes?

MUSIC STORE

I'm looking for a ...	Je cherche ...
...CD.	...un CD.
...cassette.	...une cassette.

Where is the ... section?	Où est la section ...
...jazz...	...jazz?
...classical...	...classique?
...soundtracks...	...des bandes sonores?
...rock...	...rock?
...rap/hip-hop...	...rap/hip-hop?
...country...	...country?
...alternative...	...alternative?
...world music...	...musique du monde?
...dance/techno...	...dance/techno?

DRUGSTORE

May I speak with a pharmacist?
Est-ce que je peux parler à un pharmacien?

Which product do you recommend?
Quel produit me recommandez-vous?

I'm looking for ...	**Je cherche ...**
...aftershave.	**...de la lotion après-rasage.**
...antihistamines.	**...des antihistaminiques.**
...aspirin.	**...de l'aspirine.**
...band-aids.	**...des pansements.**
...bubble bath.	**...du bain moussant.**
...conditioner.	**...du revitalisant.**
...condoms.	**...des condoms.**
...dental floss.	**...de la soie dentaire.**
...deodorant.	**...du déodorant.**
...diapers.	**...des couches pour bébé.**
...disinfectant.	**...du désinfectant.**
...hand cream.	**...de la crème à mains.**
...makeup.	**...du maquillage.**
...mouthwash.	**...du rince-bouche.**
...a painkiller.	**...un analgésique.**
...perfume.	**...du parfum.**
...powder.	**...de la poudre.**
...razor blades.	**...des lames de rasoir.**
...sanitary pads.	**...des serviettes sanitaires.**
...shampoo.	**...du shampoing.**
...shaving cream.	**...de la crème à raser.**
...soap.	**...du savon.**
...sunscreen.	**...un écran solaire/ de la crème solaire.**
...tampons.	**...des tampons.**
...a toothbrush.	**...une brosse à dents.**
...toothpaste.	**...de la pâte à dents/ du dentifrice.**
...vitamins.	**...des vitamines.**

Can you give me something for ...	**Avez-vous quelque chose pour ...**
...insect bites?	**...les piqûres d'insectes?**
...an upset stomach?	**...le mal d'estomac?**
...a cold?	**...le rhume?**
...a cough?	**...la toux?**
...a headache?	**...le mal de tête?**
...a sore throat?	**...le mal de gorge?**
...hay fever?	**...le rhume des foins/ la fièvre des foins?**
...diarrhea?	**...la diarrhée?**

Do I need a prescription?
Ai-je besoin d'une ordonnance?

PHOTO SHOP

Can you develop this film please?
Pouvez-vous développer ce film, s'il vous plaît?

When will the photos be ready?
Quand les photos seront-elles prêtes?

I need a roll of film for this camera.
J'ai besoin d'un film pour cet appareil photo.

Black and white
Noir et blanc

Color
Couleur

AT THE DOCTOR'S OFFICE

Can I see a doctor?
Puis-je voir un médecin?

I have a fever.
Je fais de la fièvre.

I am diabetic.
Je suis diabétique.

I am allergic to penicillin.
Je suis allergique à la pénicilline.

I am asthmatic.
Je suis asthmatique.

I have a headache.
J'ai mal à la tête.

I have a rash.
J'ai des boutons.

I am dizzy.
J'ai des étourdissements.

I feel nauseous.
J'ai la nausée.

I have an upset stomach.
J'ai mal à l'estomac.

I suffer from high blood pressure.
Je fais de l'hypertension.

I am pregnant.
Je suis enceinte.

AT THE DOCTOR'S OFFICE

What are your symptoms?
Quels sont vos symptômes?

sneezing	**éternuements**
coughing	**toux**
sore throat	**gorge irritée**
stuffy nose	**nez bouché**
runny nose	**nez qui coule**
watery eyes	**yeux qui coulent**
fever	**fièvre**
hives	**urticaire**
swelling	**enflure**
headache	**mal de tête**
fatigue	**fatigue**
aches and pains	**douleur**
cramps	**crampes**
diarrhea	**diarrhée**
dizziness	**étourdissements**

Are you allergic to any medications?
Avez-vous des allergies aux médicaments?

What is your blood type?
Quel est votre groupe sanguin?

THE HUMAN BODY

ankle	**cheville**
appendix	**appendice**
arm	**bras**
armpit	**aisselle**
back	**dos**
beauty mark	**grain de beauté**
bellybutton	**nombril**
bladder	**vessie**
blood	**sang**
bone	**os**
brain	**cerveau**

AT THE DOCTOR'S OFFICE

breast	**sein**
bronchus	**bronche**
calf	**mollet**
cartilage	**cartillage**
cheek	**joue**
chest	**poitrine**
ear	**oreille**
eardrum	**tympan**
elbow	**coude**
esophagus	**œsophage**
eye	**œil** (plural: **yeux**)
eyebrow	**sourcil**
eyelash	**cil**
face	**visage**
finger	**doigt**
foot	**pied**
forehead	**front**
gallbladder	**vésicule biliaire**
hair	**cheveux**
hand	**main**
heart	**cœur**
heel	**talon**
intestine	**intestin**
kidney	**rein**
knee	**genou**
knuckle	**jointure**
liver	**foie**
lung	**poumon**
muscle	**muscle**
nail	**ongle**
neck	**cou**
nerve	**nerf**
nose	**nez**
nostril	**narine**
palate	**palais**
palm	**paume**
rib	**côte**
saliva	**salive**
shoulder	**épaule**

shoulderblade	**omoplate**
sinus	**sinus**
skin	**peau**
spine	**colonne vertébrale, colonne**
stomach	**estomac**
temple	**tempe**
tendon	**tendon**
thigh	**cuisse**
throat	**gorge**
thumb	**pouce**
toe	**orteil**
tongue	**langue**
tonsils	**amygdales**
tooth	**dent**
urinary tract	**tractus urinaire**
vein	**veine**
vertebra	**vertèbre**
waist	**taille**
windpipe	**trachée**
wrist	**poignet**

You have …	Vous avez …
…bronchitis.	**…une bronchite.**
…chicken pox.	**…la varicelle.**
…a cold.	**…un rhume.**
…diabetes.	**…le diabète.**
…an ear infection.	**…une otite.**
…the flu.	**…la grippe.**
…food poisoning.	**…un empoisonnement alimentaire.**
…hay fever.	**…la fièvre des foins.**
…high blood pressure.	**…de la haute pression.**
…laryngitis.	**…une laryngite.**
…meningitis.	**…la méningite.**
…a migraine.	**…une migraine.**
…pneumonia.	**…une pneumonie.**

…the stomach flu.	**…une gastro/ gastro-entérite.**
…an ulcer.	**…un ulcère.**
…a urinary-tract infection.	**…une infection urinaire.**

Can you write me a prescription?
Pouvez-vous me prescrire quelque chose?

painkillers	**anti-inflammatoires**
antibiotics	**antibiotiques**
penicillin	**pénicilline**
cough syrup	**sirop pour la toux**
eyedrops	**gouttes pour les yeux**
ear drops	**gouttes pour les oreilles**

AT THE BANK

I would like to exchange some money/traveler's
checks.
**J'aimerais changer de l'argent/des chèques
de voyage.**

What is the exchange rate?
Quel est le taux de change?

Can I use my credit card to withdraw some
money?
**Est-ce que je peux retirer de l'argent avec
ma carte de crédit?**

account	**compte**
ATM card	**carte de guichet**
balance	**solde**
check	**chèque**
checking account	**compte chèque**
credit	**crédit**
credit card	**carte de crédit**
debit	**débit**
deposit	**dépôt**
exchange rate	**taux de change**
interest rate	**taux d'intérêt**
loan	**prêt**
mortgage	**hypothèque**
savings account	**compte d'épargne**
traveler's check	**chèque de voyage**
withdrawal	**retrait**

AT THE POST OFFICE

I would like to buy stamps.
J'aimerais acheter des timbres.

How much is it to send a postcard/letter to the
United States?
**C'est combien pour envoyer une carte
postale/lettre aux États-Unis?**

When will it arrive?
Quand cela arrivera-t-il?

air mail	**par avion**
envelope	**enveloppe**
letter	**lettre**
mail	**courrier**
mailbox	**boîte aux lettres**
mailman	**facteur**
package	**colis**
postcard	**carte postale**
post office	**bureau de poste**
registered mail	**courrier recommandé**
stamp	**timbre**

HOLIDAYS

New Year's Day (Jan. 1)	**Jour de l'An/Nouvel An**
Valentine's Day (Feb. 14)	**Saint-Valentin**
St. Patrick's Day (Mar. 17)	**Saint-Patrick**
Easter (varies)	**Pâques**
April Fool's Day (Apr. 1)	**Poisson d'avril**
Mother's Day (2nd Sun. in May)	**Fête des Mères**
Victoria Day (Mon. before May 25)	**Fête de la Reine**
Father's Day (3rd Sun. in June)	**Fête des Pères**
St. Jean Baptiste Day (June 24)	**Saint-Jean-Baptiste**
Canada Day (July 1)	**Fête du Canada**
Labor Day (1st Mon. in Sept.)	**Fête du Travail**
Thanksgiving (2nd Mon. in Oct.)	**Action de Grâces**
Halloween (Oct. 31)	**Halloween**
Remembrance Day (Nov. 11)	**Jour du Souvenir**
Christmas (Dec. 25)	**Noël**
Boxing Day (Dec. 26)	**Lendemain de Noël/ Boxing Day**

HOLIDAYS

- Victoria Day: Canadian holiday established in 1845 to celebrate the birthday of Queen Victoria.

- St. Jean Baptiste Day: feast day of St. John the Baptist, patron saint of French Canadians. Also called *Fête nationale*. This holiday celebrates Quebec culture (provincial holiday).

- Canada Day: Canada's national holiday celebrating the establishment of the Dominion of Canada on July 1, 1867.

- Remembrance Day: day honoring the memory of Canadians killed in wars in which Canada has been involved.

- Boxing Day: day after Christmas named after the practice of giving "boxes" or presents to employees, mailmen, etc. This day is known for its after-Christmas sales.

TIME & DATES

TELLING THE TIME

What time is it?
Quelle heure est-il?

It's ... o'clock.
Il est ... heure(s).

It is 2:30.
Il est deux heures et demie.

It is a quarter past three.
Il est trois heures et quart.

It is a quarter to three.
Il est trois heures moins quart.

It is 20 past three.
Il est trois heures et vingt.

It is 20 to three.
Il est trois heures moins vingt.

| early | **tôt** |
| late | **tard** |

morning	**matin**
afternoon	**après-midi**
evening	**soirée**
night	**soir**

TIME & DATES

DAYS OF THE WEEK

Monday	**lundi**
Tuesday	**mardi**
Wednesday	**mercredi**
Thursday	**jeudi**
Friday	**vendredi**
Saturday	**samedi**
Sunday	**dimanche**

MONTHS

January	**janvier**
February	**février**
March	**mars**
April	**avril**
May	**mai**
June	**juin**
July	**juillet**
August	**août**
September	**septembre**
October	**octobre**
November	**novembre**
December	**décembre**

SEASONS

fall	**automne**
spring	**printemps**
summer	**été**
winter	**hiver**

WEIGHTS & MEASURES

centimeter	**centimètre**
foot	**pied**
inch	**pouce**
kilogram	**kilo/kilogramme**
kilometer	**kilomètre**
liter	**litre**
meter	**mètre**
mile	**mille**
pound	**livre**

1 mile = 1.609 kilometer (km)
1 kilometer = 0.621 mile

1 US gallon = 3.78 liters (l)
1 liter = 0.26 gallon

1 inch = 2.54 centimeters (cm)
1 centimeter = 0.39 inch

1 foot = 0.305 meter (m)
1 meter = 39.4 inches

1 pound = 454 grams (g) = 0.45 kilogram (kg)
1 kilogram = 2.2 pounds

USEFUL WORDS

a little	**un peu**
a dozen	**une douzaine**
a few	**quelques**
less	**moins**
many	**beaucoup**
more	**plus**
too much	**trop**
not enough	**pas assez**

NUMBERS

one	un
two	deux
three	trois
four	quatre
five	cinq
six	six
seven	sept
eight	huit
nine	neuf
ten	dix
eleven	onze
twelve	douze
thirteen	treize
fourteen	quatorze
fifteen	quinze
sixteen	seize
seventeen	dix-sept
eighteen	dix-huit
nineteen	dix-neuf
twenty	vingt
thirty	trente
forty	quarante
fifty	cinquante
sixty	soixante
seventy	soixante-dix
eighty	quatre-vingts
ninety	quatre-vingt-dix
one hundred	cent
one thousand	mille
one million	un million
one billion	un milliard

ORDINALS

1st	first	**premier**
2nd	second	**deuxième**
3rd	third	**troisième**
4th	fourth	**quatrième**
5th	fifth	**cinquième**
Xth		**énième**

FRACTIONS

a half	**un demi**
a quarter	**un quart**
a third	**un tiers**
a tenth	**un dixième**
three-quarters	**trois quarts**
15%	**quinze pour cent**
double	**le double**
half	**la moitié**

COLORS

beige	**beige**
black	**noir**
blue	**bleu**
bronze	**bronze**
brown	**brun, marron**
burgundy	**bourgogne**
copper	**cuivre**
eggplant	**aubergine**
fuschia	**fuschia**
gold	**or**
gray	**gris**
green	**vert**
khaki	**kaki**
light	**pâle**
lilac	**lilas**
navy	**marine, bleu marin**
off-white	**blanc cassé**
orange	**orange**
pastel	**pastel**
pink	**rose**
purple	**mauve**
red	**rouge; roux** (hair)
royal blue	**bleu royal**
silver	**argent**
turquoise	**turquoise**
violet	**violet**
white	**blanc**
yellow	**jaune**

QUÉBÉCOIS EXPRESSIONS*

Arrive en ville!
(Arrive in the city)
Welcome to the 21st century!

Attraper son coup de mort
(To catch one's death)
To catch one's death

Accrocher ses patins
(To hang up one's skates)
To hang up one's skates

En avoir plein le casque
(To have one's helmet full)
To have had enough

Frapper un nœud
(To hit a knot)
To hit a snag

Tomber dans l'œil
(To fall into someone's eye)
To catch someone's eye

Être bleu marin/Être bleu marin noir
(To be navy blue/To be navy blue black)
To be very angry

Se faire chanter la pomme
(To have one's apple sung to)
To be hit on

Se faire des accraires/Se faire des accroires
(To make oneself believe things)
To delude oneself

*Expressions noted in parentheses are the literal translations of the French expressions.

Être fait à l'os
(To be done to the bone)
　　To be toast

En arracher
(To uproot)
　　To have difficulty

Avoir son voyage
(To have one's trip)
　　To have had enough

Avoir un kick sur quelqu'un
(To have a kick on someone)
　　To have a crush on someone

Se pogner le bacon
(To hold on to one's bacon)
　　To twiddle one's thumbs

Se sucrer le bec
(To sweeten one's mouth)
　　To eat something sweet

Avoir l'air bête
(To look like a beast)
　　To be grumpy

Avoir les yeux dans la graisse de binnes
(To have one's eyes in bean grease)
　　To be in a daze

Avoir un air de bœufs/Avoir une face de bœufs
(To look like an ox/To have the face of an ox)
　　To be grumpy

Bonhomme sept heures
(Seven o'clock man)
　　Boogeyman

Dans le boutte
(In the end)
  In the area

C'est au boutte!
(It's in the end)
  Awesome!

Avoir le gros boutte du bâton
(To have the big end of the stick)
  To have the big end of the stick

Prendre une brosse
(To take a brush)
  To get drunk

Ça vient de s'éteindre!
(It has just been extinguished)
  The last ray of hope has gone out

Être dans le champs/Être dans les patates
(To be in the field/To be in the potatoes)
  To be out in left field

Être habillé comme la chienne à Jacques
(To be dressed like Jacques' dog)
  To be poorly dressed/To be inappropriately
    dressed

Avoir la chienne
(To have the dog)
  To be scared

Son chien est mort!
(His dog is dead)
  It will never happen.

Faire la commande
(To do the order)
  To go grocery shopping

Avoir passé la nuit sur la corde à linge
(To have spent the night on the clothesline)
   To have had a rough night

S'énerver le poil des jambes
(To excite the hair on one's legs)
   To get excited/To panic

Être au coton
(To be at the cotton)
   To be exhausted

Être crampé
(To be cramped)
   To be rolling on the floor laughing

Dormir sur la switch
(To sleep on the switch)
   Asleep at the wheel

Enweille!
(—————)
   Come on!

S'en ficher comme de l'an quarante
(To care about it as much as for the year 1940)
   To not give a rat's ass

Être fou comme un balai
(To be crazy like a broom)
   To be completely excited about something

Être game
(To be game)
   To be game

Se faire griller/bronzer
(To grill/bronze oneself)
   To sunbathe

Être dans le jus
(To be in the juice)
  To have a lot on one's plate

Donner un lift
(To give a lift)
  To give a ride

Manger ses bas
(To eat one's socks)
  To be worried

En masse
(En masse)
  A lot

Il y a du monde à la messe
(There are lots of people at Mass)
  Tons of people are here

Se prendre pour le nombril du monde
(To think of oneself as the bellybutton of the
  world)
  To think one is the center of the universe

Ça prend pas la tête à Papineau!
(It doesn't take Papineau's head)
  No need to be a rocket scientist!

Lâche pas la patate!
(Don't let go of the potato)
  Don't give up!

Pis ça?
(And so?)
  So what?

Être de bonne heure sur le piton
(To be early on the button)
  To be up early

Pogner les nerfs
(To catch the nerves)
  To become frustrated

Sirop de poteau
(Telephone pole syrup)
  Artificial pancake syrup
    (i.e. not real maple syrup)

Tiguidou!
(———————)
  Perfect!

Tourlou!
(———————)
  Toodle-oo!

Faire du train
(To make some train)
  To make a lot of noise

Avoir les deux yeux dans le même trou
(To have both eyes in the same eye socket)
  To be cross-eyed

Boire comme un trou
(To drink like a hole)
  To drink like a fish

Tsé-veut-dire?
(Know what I mean?)
  Know what I mean?

Attache ta tuque!
(Tie up your hat)
  Hold on to your hat!

Ça a pas d'allure
(It has no manner)
  It doesn't make sense/It's impossible

Faire la baboune
(To make a baboon face)
   To sulk

Être d'adon
(————————)
   To be easy to live with

Rester bête
(To stay like a beast)
   To be stunned

Ne pas être du monde
(To not be people)
   To have no manners

Sacrer son camp
(To swear one's camp)
   To get out of here

C'est pas vargeux!
(————————)
   Nothing great!

Parler à travers son chapeau
(To talk through one's hat)
   To talk through one's hat

Le chat est sorti du sac
(The cat is out of the bag)
   The cat is out of the bag

Manquer le bateau
(To miss the boat)
   The ship has sailed

J'capote!
(————————)
   I'm going out of my mind!

Capoter sur quelqu'un
(—————)
   To have a crush on somebody

Être cassé
(To be broken)
   To be broke

Virer fou
(To turn crazy)
   To go crazy

Faire le frais
(To do the fresh)
   To show off

Arrête de lambiner!
(—————)
   Stop wasting your time!

Arrête de niaiser!
(—————)
   Stop fooling around!

Prendre une débarque
(—————)
   To fall

C'est 'ben gonzo!
(It's really gonzo)
   It's really stupid!

REFERENCES

Dagenais, Gérard. *Dictionnaire des difficultés de la langue française au Canada*, 2nd ed. Boucherville: Les éditions françaises, 1990.

Grévisse, Maurice. *Précis de grammaire française*, 30th ed. Paris: Duculot, 1995.

Office de la langue française. *Canadianismes de bon aloi*. Quebec City: Ministère de l'Éducation du Québec, 1973.

Therrien, Michel. *Code grammatical en tableaux*. Montreal: Brault et Bouthillier, 1991.